TURKMENISTAN

MaryLee Knowlton

MARSHALL **C**AVENDISH **B**ENCHMARK

NEW YORK

PICTURE CREDITS

Cover: © Nevada Wier/Corbis

Bes Stock: 137 • The Bridgeman Art Library: 65 • Camera Press: 33, 46, 47, 50, 80, 83 • Christopher Herwig Photography: 1, 5, 6, 58, 71, 84, 124, 127 • Corbis, Inc.: 7, 12, 18, 21, 25, 26, 27, 40, 48, 53, 68, 77, 81, 82, 85, 86, 90, 99, 100, 101, 103, 108, 126, 128 • Eye Ubiquitous / Hutchison Library: 14, 60, 62, 63, 88 • Getty Images: 8, 66, 75, 109, 117 • Hans Rossel Photography: 11, 19, 35, 61, 102, 113 • Lonely Planet Images: 15, 17, 20, 22, 23, 34, 59, 67, 78 • Reuters: 36, 38, 43, 44, 49, 64, 74, 76, 87, 114, 116, 118, 119, 120, 121, 122, 125 • Audrius Tomonis / www.banknotes.com: 135 • Topfoto: 24, 31, 42, 56 • Travel Images: 3, 4, 9, 13, 16, 28, 29, 30, 32, 37, 39, 41, 52, 54, 57, 69, 72, 91, 92, 93, 94, 96, 98, 105, 106, 111, 112, 123, 129

PRECEDING PAGE

A young Turkmen girl piggybacks her little brother in the heat of the Kara-Kum Desert.

Marshall Cavendish Benchmark
99 White Plains Road
Tarrytown, NY 10591
Website: www.marshallcavendish.us

© Marshall Cavendish International (Asia) Private Limited 2006
® "Cultures of the World" is a registered trademark of Times Publishing Limited.

Series concept and design by Times Editions
An imprint of Marshall Cavendish International (Asia) Private Limited
A member of Times Publishing Limited

Library of Congress Cataloging-in-Publication Data
Knowlton, MaryLee, 1946–
    Turkmenistan / by MaryLee Knowlton.—1st ed.
        p. cm.—(Cultures of the world)
    Includes bibliographical references and index.
    ISBN 0-7614-2014-2
    1. Turkmenistan—Juvenile literature. I. Title. II. Series.
    DK933.K58 2006
    958.5—dc22   2005006455

Printed in China

7 6 5 4 3 2 1

CONTENTS

The Rukhiyet Conventions and Arts Palace in Ashkhabad.

The Turabes Khanyn Mausoleum at Konye Urgench.

INTRODUCTION

TURKMENISTAN IS ONE OF THE WORLD'S newest nations, carved out of the desert lands of central Asia by the Russians and liberated when the Soviet Union collapsed in the early 1990s. At the same time, it is one of the world's oldest cultures, a collection of nomadic peoples whose adjustment to life in the desert has spanned centuries as well as miles.

Since declaring independence in 1991, Turkmenistan has been under the unpredictable and totalitarian rule of the man who calls himself Turkmenbashi, the father of all Turkmens. Under his guidance, the economy has faltered and the country has become increasingly isolated from its neighbors and other potential allies. Still, as they did throughout the Soviet-dominated 20th century, the Turkmen people face the challenges of the new century with resilience and determination.

GEOGRAPHY

TURKMENISTAN IS THE SOUTHERNMOST of the Soviet Union's former republics, a land slightly larger than the state of California. It lies to the east of the Caspian Sea, with which it has its longest border, 1,098 miles (1,768 km). It shares its southern borders with Iran (616 miles, or 992 km) and Afghanistan (462 miles, or 744 km). Uzbekistan lies to the north and east with a 1,006-mile (1,619-km) border, and Kazakhstan lies to the north, sharing the border with Turkmenistan for 235 miles (379 km). These borders did not exist until the 20th century when the Russians, in their acquisition of the land and their creation of the various republics that made up their confederation, found it politically convenient to have

Opposite: **The climate varies and temperatures fluctuate in different parts of the vast expanse of desert found in Turkmenistan.**

Below: **A Turkmen boy watches over his herd of horses as they graze in an oasis overshadowed by the Kopet-Dag mountain range.**

One-humped Arvana dromedary camels are a common sight in the "Black Sand," as the harsh Kara-Kum Desert has come to be known.

established borders. To that end, the central Asian republics were created, initially in 1924–25, although boundaries and official designations shifted and were altered somewhat through the mid-1930s. The residents of Uzbekistan, Kazakhstan, and Turkmenistan had nothing to say about the matter, while their nations were being brought into official existence by the Soviet leadership. The people living in what became Turkmenistan, as well as in large parts of the countries it bordered, were mostly nomadic, and establishing borders cut many of them off from either their summer or their winter pastures.

Almost all of Turkmenistan is desert or steppe. The sands of the Kara-Kum Desert cover 80 percent of the nation's total landmass of 188,407 square miles (488,000 square km). Most of the people live in oasis settlements in the southern shadow of the Kopet-Dag mountain range or along Turkmenistan's three main rivers: the Murgab, the Tedzhen, and the Amu Darya.

STEPPE

The Russian word *step*, which describes the lands of Siberia, has become a part of the English language, though spelled *steppe*. It refers to a semiarid area of land where grass grows or once did. Steppes fall into three categories. Wooded steppe receives more than 16 inches (41 cm) of precipitation annually, enough to support tree life. Tillable steppe is made of fertile black soil and gets 10 to 15 inches (25 to 38 cm) of annual rainfall. Native grasses—ideal for grazing livestock—thrive, and irrigation allows for continuing productive agriculture as it does in the wheat belts of the United States and Russia. Finally, there is the nontillable steppe, which receives less than 10 inches (25 cm) of rain per year.

Vast stretches of steppe add to the dry, often harsh conditions that prevail in Turkmenistan.

In Turkmenistan the land generally falls into the third and least hospitable category of steppe. Nontillable, or semi-desert, conditions prevail. The lives and livelihoods of the people of Turkmenistan have been shaped by the adaptations they have made to the demands of this challenging environment.

THE KARA-KUM DESERT

Opposite: **Against the backdrop of a near barren stretch of the vast Kara-Kum Desert, this young girl poses with one of the village camels.**

The Kara-Kum Desert is called the *Garagum* in Turkmen, meaning "Black Sand." Stretching 500 miles (805 km) from west to east and 300 miles (483 km) from north to south, its 135,000 square miles (349,650 square km) constitute 70 percent of the entire land area of Turkmenistan. This sprawling region is located to the west of the Caspian Sea and south of the Aral Sea and the Amu Darya River. Its southern border is formed by the Kopet-Dag Mountains. To its northeast lies another desert, the Kyzyl Kum. The little water that is found there naturally flows from the Hindu Kush Mountains, which lie to the south of the desert, where the Murgab and Tedzhen rivers provide irrigation water.

A CLOSE SHAVE

Wild Turkmen horses known as *kulans-onagers* have reportedly escaped a close brush with extinction. A wildlife reserve in Badkhiz reported that a small herd of *kulans-onagers* had multiplied to reach a size of more than 7,300 horses in the mid-1990s, though the population has dwindled since. This is a surprising and welcome development since, in the 1930s, the known number of wild horses in Turkmenistan was about 250. It was feared at the time that the species would disappear entirely. A reserve of 216,570 acres (87,680 hectares) was created between the Murgab and Tedzhen rivers to provide a sanctuary for these distinctive and distinctly Turkmen animals.

The Kara-Kum has three distinct parts. Each has its own climate, though throughout the entire region, summers are generally long, hot, and very dry. The northern part of the desert is called the Trans-Unguz Kara-Kum, where the summers are the coolest—ranging from 79 to 82°F (26 to 28°C)—and the rainfall the scarcest—only 2.75 inches (7 cm) a year. The average winter temperature is 25°F (-4°C), but in the Trans-Unguz Kara-Kum and in the desert as a whole it can fluctuate more than 50°F (28°C) on any given day.

FLORA AND FAUNA

Animals and plants are not plentiful in the Kara-Kum, but they are varied. In April the desert blooms, and for a few short weeks it is alive with flowering plants whose bright reds, yellows, and oranges enliven the landscape. Fruit thrives in the oasis and irrigated areas and is especially plentiful in the fall.

Oases located near both the city and province of Mary and the Tedzhen region have made these areas critical to Turkmenistan's cotton crop. Their commercial legacy can be traced back several centuries. They were once important stops for traders following the Silk Road, the vast network that connected Europe and Asia

The Kara-Kum Canal, a Soviet initiative, channels water from the Amu Darya River to irrigate nearby fields. The canal has brought with it not only much needed water, but also significant socio-economic and ecological changes.

and provided a thoroughfare for the exchange and spread of not only products but also ideas.

The Soviets recognized the importance of the Kara-Kum as a source of minerals in the second half of the 20th century and conducted archaeological and geographical studies to determine if it was suitable for other purposes. Transportation and irrigation emerged as specific areas in need of further development.

In 1954 the USSR began construction of the world's largest irrigation canal. Since its completion in 1967, the Kara-Kum Canal has watered the desert, running 520 miles (837 km) from the Amu Darya River to Geok-Tepe, a former fortress in the oasis of Akhal-tekke. Beginning in the 1970s, further construction extended the canal to the Caspian Sea, and today it is more that 870 miles (1,400 km) long. Nearly 300 miles (483 km) are navigable (wide and deep enough to be used by ships), though its main function is irrigation.

As engineers and geographers studied the desert for practical purposes, archaeologists conducted expeditions that resulted in important historical discoveries. Near the Geoksyur Oasis, scientists found that the canal the government was building was not the first to be constructed in the desert. They unearthed, from deep beneath the sands, the remains of canals dating from 3000 to 2000 B.C. The dry desert sands had also preserved buildings, artifacts, and written documents from the same period near the capital, Ashkhabad. Outside Dzheytun archaeologists have discovered the remains of what many believe is the earliest agricultural settlement in west-central Asia.

Since World War II, the Kara-Kum has become increasingly industrialized as factories and railroads have been built, oil and gas pipelines laid, and power stations erected. Where most people once lived as nomads, towns

These ancient ruins bear witness to the rich cultures that temporarily settled in the current Turkmen region.

have arisen, fully supplied with electricity and gas. Irrigation has enabled the cultivation of cotton, fruit, and vegetable crops not only around the oases but also well beyond.

THE ARAL SEA

Throughout the Soviet years, the Aral Sea's waters figured critically in various five-year agricultural and economic plans. Over the course of nearly 50 years, the rivers that flow into the sea were drained to supply irrigation for the surrounding desert lands, effectively transforming these into fertile and productive fields. The effect of this activity has been nothing short of catastrophic not only for the Aral Sea but also for the biodiversity and inhabitants of the region, as well as the ecological system as a whole.

THE ARVANA DROMEDARY

For thousands of years, Turkmens have relied on the camel for milk, wool, and transportation between their summer pastures and their winter homes. The Arvana dromedary has been the Turkmens' prized breed for nearly 1,000 years. They are known, and specially bred, for their high yields of milk, a smooth ride, and the ability to carry heavy loads. They are raised across Turkmenistan as well as in Uzbekistan, Azerbaijan, Kazakhstan, Turkey, northern Iran, and Afghanistan.

The Arvana is not the more familiar swift long-legged beast found in the deserts of Saudi Arabia. Rather, it is a short, relatively slow animal, whose value lies in its ability to go without water and with little food for long periods of time. Also, it matures quickly. Females can bear two calves in three years, making it easier and more economical to increase their herd size.

A monument in Ash-khabad dedicated to the victims of the catas-trophic earthquake that devastated the capital in 1948.

EARTHQUAKES

At the end of the 19th and beginning of the 20th centuries, Turkmenistan was repeatedly plagued by earthquakes—in 1893, 1895, 1924, and 1929. Then, in 1948, it was hit by one of the 10 deadliest earthquakes in recorded history.

On October 5, 1948, an earthquake measuring 7.3 on the Richter scale struck Turkmenistan in the area around Ashkhabad. The city was completely destroyed. At the time, Turkmenistan was part of the Soviet Union. As part of Stalin's policy of secrecy, accounts of the earthquake marginalized the scale of the damage and underreported the number of people killed. Although it was reported then that 35,000 people had died in the massive earthquake, the real number was closer to 176,000,

nearly 90 percent of the population of Ashkhabad. Communist party functionaries closed the city to outsiders for more than a year. Nearly five years passed before all the bodies of the victims were recovered from the rubble and ruins.

Today a monument and a museum, both in Ashkhabad, have been dedicated to the victims of the tragedy, and January 12 is known as Remembrance Day and is observed as a national day of mourning in their honor. A cemetery in the northern part of the city holds the remains of the dead. The mother and two brothers of Turkmenistan's president Saparmurat Niyazov had also died in the earthquake. They were initially buried in the earthquake cemetery, but in 2004 the president had his mother's, as well as his father's, remains dug up. They were buried again in another part of the country in a two-day televised spectacle.

In this Ashkhabad monument, the bull shaking the globe in its horns symbolically represents the earthquake that killed President Saparmurat Niyazov's beloved mother, leaving him as one of the tragedy's few survivors. Peering down from above is one of the many portraits of the leader that can be found hanging in various parts of the capital.

THE YURT: MAKING THE BEST OF A DIFFICULT SITUATION

Traditionally, nomadic Turkmens had to be able to pack up, move everything they owned, and set up home in another location at least twice a year. Living alternately in areas of extreme heat and cold, they needed shelter that would suit both climates and that was easy to transport. The land had few trees that could supply lumber for building houses, and stone and mud bricks were too heavy to be moved from place to place. All these contributed to the creation of the yurt: a structure that can withstand strong winds and whose felt walls become more waterproof with increased exposure to the rain.

The yurt (*below*), a circular tent built of felted wool fitted onto a lattice frame, has been the home of the nomads of central Asia from Mongolia to Anatolia (part of modern-day Turkey) since as early as 600 B.C. The structure consists of a round frame made of flexible trellis sides, a door on one side, a set of curved struts (pieces that provide support and resist pressure) attached to the sides, and a wheel that rests on the top of the struts as they curve toward the center of the tent. Layers of felt are anchored onto the frame by yards of woven tent bands that surround the tent both inside and out. The center of the tent is left open at the top, allowing smoke to escape and fresh air to circulate as needed.

When setting up a yurt, the Turkmens first set up the walls, then the struts, and finally the wheel at the top. They drape and tie felts to the struts, leaving the wheel or roof open. The

wheel is then covered with one last piece of felt that will be folded back whenever necessary to adjust the temperature inside the yurt. Lastly they hang another layer of four rectangular felts over the sides of the tent. The doorway is formed by a flap or, in more elaborate yurts, a double wooden door. Ideally the door faces south.

The smoke hole in the roof is left open all summer but is closed during the rest of the year. Positioned slightly to the front of the yurt, the smoke hole admits the light from the southern sun. The inside of the tent is brightened as the light shifts with the sun's direction in the sky during the day, creating a sundial of sorts that tells when it is time for prayers. When the weather is hot, cooking is done outside the yurt. The tent sides are also often raised at the bottom, so that air can circulate. In the winter, when a fire is needed for heat and for cooking, it is built in the center of the tent and is vented through the smoke hole.

Besides housing for nomadic Turkmens, the yurt also traditionally served as an elaborate temporary location for special events taking place in settled communities. Persian paintings of travelers from the 15th and 16th centuries show yurts fit for nobility, their sides studded with gems and silver and draped with luxurious carpets rich in pattern and design.

HISTORY

TURKMENISTAN'S HISTORY PRIOR to the 20th century is an account of an area and a people, but not of a nation. Until the 1920s Turkmenistan had no established borders with neighboring regions, no central economy or government, and no distinct national identity. Ruled and contested by legendary empires led by Genghis Khan, Tamerlane, and Alexander the Great, the area's long tradition of tribal governance and clan loyalties served its people well until the pervasive and often all-consuming rule of the Soviets was established.

Above: **Archaeological ruins and ancient mosques and palaces bear witness to the region's storied past.**

Opposite: **The mesmerizing interior of an old mosque In Turkmenistan.**

The earliest history of the Turkmen people is not contained in written records or in oral accounts passed down through the generations. It is reflected in the archaeological remains that offer glimpses into the lives of the inhabitants of the earliest settlements and encampments. The climate of central Asia may have made the region inhospitable to settlement, but its sand and relatively dry conditions have also preserved evidence of how and where people once lived. Scientific advances such as carbon-14 dating have solved even more mysteries about the region's earliest and most successful initial settlers.

Scholars disagree about where the first people to settle in central Asia, and in particular the area then known as Turkistan, came from. Nevertheless they do agree that these first residents were probably nomadic goat herders. Occupying caves for part of the year and yurts that they moved as and when necessary during other parts of the year, they left traces of their existence on cave walls and under shifting sands to be discovered centuries later. In around 6000 B.C. some of the region's inhabitants began to construct settlements out of simple mud bricks.

A Turkmen farmer on the road with his donkey, with the 13th-century Kutlug Timur minaret (left) and the 14th-century Sultan Takesh Mausoleum, evidence of centuries of foreign aggression, looming in the background.

In the southwestern part of what is today Turkmenistan, in the area called Geok-Tepe, remains of palaces, public buildings, and irrigation canals testify to the existence of large urban areas from as early as the 15th century B.C. In the centuries that followed, conquests and increased trade contacts with the outside world changed life in these expanding urban centers. Generally, however, the culture seems to have altered little, continuing as it had for more than 5,000 years. Within this culture, three patterns of living emerged: nomadic, pastoralist, and settled.

EARLY NOMADS, PASTORALISTS, AND SETTLERS

Nomads maintained temporary settlements in more than one place. Their settlements were not unplanned, however. Based on how they fed, clothed, and housed themselves, they sought out and returned to the same locations year after year. Nomads fell into two categories. Hunters and gatherers made up the first group. Their movements were based on the need to find places for seasonal hunting and harvesting in areas where they could endure the extremes of the climate. Herders—breeders of domesticated animals—formed the second group. They moved primarily to find pastureland for their animals, on which they depended for food, shelter, and clothing.

Pastoralists lived in small villages where permanent houses provided shelter for individual families. The land surrounding the village was used to grow food for the villagers and their animals, but it was primarily used as pastureland. Though pastoralists did some farming, primarily raising grains, they relied mostly on their animals for their food and other needs, much as the herding nomads had done. Even though the pastoralists had permanent dwellings, they moved to the mountains in the summer, when the heat in the mud houses became unbearable and the animals did not have enough water. In the mountains, they lived in yurts that they dismantled and brought back with them to the lowlands until the next summer.

While nomads and pastoralists had at least two locations that could provide the subsistence-level economy they needed, people in the settlements had to make a living solely in one place. Most settlements were agriculturally based, which restricted their location and placement to the delta plains of the Amu Darya, Gorgan, and Atrek rivers. There,

Many Turkmens have preserved their nomadic lifestyle despite the wars and foreign oppression that have marked the past.

villagers developed irrigation systems that enabled them to produce enough food for their own consumption as well as for trade with neighboring villages. One of the region's villages eventually became a bustling city where people developed crafts and services that they could trade with neighboring villages and migrating nomads for raw materials and animals.

Though the lands that lay to the east of the Caspian Sea could boast of 300 days of sunshine a year, the accompanying heat and drought never made the area attractive to conquerors as a permanent place to settle. Nevertheless the region was important from ancient times as a route to more desirable and hospitable destinations. As such, it experienced the ravages and onslaughts of many invaders. From 600 B.C., it was part of the vast Persian Empire until Alexander the Great passed through the region 250 years later on his way to India. The Greeks, who arrived in the area next, built cities and towns that would prove to be of great importance to the trade routes that united China to the East and Europe to the West in the vast network known as the Silk Road. Three hundred years later, at Nisa, near today's Ashkhabad, the

Parthians established their capital as they tried to hold back the Roman quest for lands in the east.

THE SILK ROAD

Few people traveled the full length of the Silk Road, more accurately called the Silk Roads, since many trade routes connecting China and India with Europe threaded their way across the deserts and through the mountains of central Asia. Beginning from the East in the northern Chinese city of Xi'an, as many as 800 caravans towed by camels carried silk, satin, rubies, diamonds, pearls, musk, and rhubarb. Traded sometimes at 20-mile (32-km) intervals, these goods changed hands many times before they reached the West. Loaded with commodities such as medicines, gold, grapes, pomegranates, woolen rugs, colored glass, and green and white jade from the West, the caravan would then head back to its place of origin.

Above: **The excavation of Nisa has unearthed invaluable information about the Parthians.**

Opposite: **The tomb of Sultan Sanjar at the major archaeological site and ancient city of Merv.**

Mountain ranges and desert hills such as these often proved difficult obstacles to the travelers and traders shuttling back and forth on the routes that made up the Silk Road.

Traders traveled over, around, and through mountain ranges, skirting the deserts when they could and crossing them only if they had to. Towns grew up and thrived in the deserts around the more hospitable oases. The legendary city of Merv established itself as an important stop, and its ruins are found near present-day Mary.

Rather than describe the Silk Road by geographical distance, traders found it more useful to describe it in terms of travel time: by camel the Silk Road was a six-month journey from east to west and a trip of one month or more from north to south. Distances calculated by time allowed travelers to plan how far they would have to go not just to reach their destination, but also to replenish their food and water supplies and to find shelter. Often traders would be forced to travel for several weeks, taking with them everything they personally needed during that time in addition to the items they wished to trade. They had to plan their travels for times when they could expect to survive with no more shelter than the simple structures they could carry.

Besides material goods, travelers spread their art, food, music, and lifestyles along the Silk Road. Today, centuries later—though the area encompassed by the routes of the Silk Road includes one-seventh of the earth's surface—foods, artistic designs, and musical instruments that resemble each other appear in towns and villages spread thousands of miles apart.

THE ARRIVAL OF ISLAM

In the eighth century, Islamic forces first conquered the land that would become Turkmenistan. Though conquests and invasions had been

Classical Islamic architecture and inscriptions still exist as testament to the religion's early influence in the region that would become Turkmenistan.

occurring in the region's deserts and mountains for more than 1,200 years, they ultimately influenced the conquerors more than the Turkmens. Throughout those centuries, the native residents had continued to live as they always had, as nomads or pastoralists, raising and moving their animals and maintaining their cultural and religious traditions. The introduction of Islam and its religious and political domination began to change the social conditions of the region's inhabitants.

By the 11th century, tribes of Turkmens had begun to migrate west from their mountain homes to settle, at least for part of the year, near the Caspian Sea. At that time, this area was ruled by the Turks. Subsequently, under the leadership of Genghis Khan, the Mongols conquered the Turks in the 13th century. For the next 200 years, the Mongols ruled the land

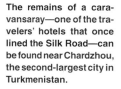

The remains of a caravansaray—one of the travelers' hotels that once lined the Silk Road—can be found near Chardzhou, the second-largest city in Turkmenistan.

until they too were expelled, this time by an Uzbek invasion of the area. Until the mid-19th century, this area, known then as Turkmenia, was ruled by two khanates, or Islamic kingdoms, Khiva and Bukhara. In 1873 Russia incorporated the khanate of Khiva into its empire to improve its own access to the trade routes of central Asia.

RUSSIAN RULE

Throughout the centuries, the Turkmens had remained nomads, loyal to none and enemy to almost everyone. Their reputation as kidnappers and outlaws ensured that no one took seriously their claims to their lands and caused those who had been victimized by their banditry to support the Russian invaders.

Turkmen resistance to the encroachment of the Russians was the strongest of any that was mobilized in central Asia. However, by the end of the 19th century, the Russian empire was firmly established. In 1869 a

The port city of Turkmen-bashi lies on the eastern shore of the Caspian Sea. Today, in addition to being the final stop at one end of the Trans-Caspian Railway, it is an important industrial area where many shipyards and other vital facilities are located.

29

port on the Caspian Sea, known today as Turkmenbashi, was founded. From there, Russian soldiers conducted raids against Turkmen settlements, slaughtering people and destroying their property and animals. The definitive defeat of the Turkmen tribes came in 1881, when the Russians captured their last stronghold, Geok-Tepe, northwest of Ashkhabad.

More than 7,000 Turkmens died in the battle for the city, and another 8,000 were massacred as they fled into the desert. Today the battle is marked by a national day of mourning each year, and the resistance the Turkmens mounted is often cited as a source of great national pride. The Russians continued their attacks by moving on to Merv and Ashkhabad, following the orders of a general whose motto was: "The harder you hit them, the longer they'll stay down." The approach proved effective, and by 1894 all the land reaching to the Caspian Sea belonged to the czar. In 1897 agreements with Afghanistan and Persia established the borders with these countries, and the Russian annexation of Turkmenistan was complete.

Throughout this period, Turkmenistan was often ruled by corrupt military officers and Russian administrators. Cities began to grow as

Russians moved into the area, and the railroads linked them to cities in other Russian colonies. Nomads, in particular, found their lifestyle difficult to sustain as Russian settlers poured into the countryside, seizing pastureland and converting it into farmland for the cultivation of crops.

In 1917 the Russian empire became the Soviet Union, and by the 1920s Turkmenistan became the Turkmen Soviet Socialist Republic. The Soviets launched plans to reform all of central Asia. In the 1930s Joseph Stalin implemented a radical new policy throughout the republic as he forced Turkmens onto large collective, or group, farms, seizing their pastureland and destroying their herds. Throughout central Asia, famine became as familiar as the nomadic lifestyle had once been. Turkmens fled to Iran and Afghanistan or into the Kara-Kum Desert. By 1936, in their effort to preserve their nomadic way of life, more than a million Turkmens had become refugees in the desert or in neighboring countries. Many of their descendants remain there today.

Until the 1991 collapse of the Soviet Union, Turkmenistan was ruled from Moscow. However, its remote and far-flung communities were less affected than the more

Old men reminisce in a town square. The past serves not only as an inspiration but also as a powerful reminder of the various struggles the Turkmen people have faced.

urbanized Russia by Moscow's cultural policies. Still, the Soviet cultural machine reduced the influence of family and tribal loyalties, redefining them as old-fashioned and unprogressive. Russians were installed in all important government offices, and Russian became Turkmenistan's official language. Religious practices were also discouraged to the point of nearly disappearing. In the late 1980s democratic reform movements swept through many of the satellite republics and the whole of the Soviet Union itself. However, their effects stopped short of Turkmenistan, where the entrenched Communist Party survived without change until it became the ruling party of the newly independent Turkmenistan in 1991. The only significant change was its new name, the Democratic Party of Turkmenistan.

INDEPENDENCE

Independent Turkmenistan has had only one ruler, Saparmurat Niyazov, whose totalitarian rule predates the changes of 1991. His domination of the government and the Turkmen people violates the laws and constitution of the country. Under his leadership, Turkmenistan has pursued a course of internal repression and international isolation, a direction the nation will apparently not swerve from anytime soon. In 1999, with the leader's encouragement and approval, the Turkmen government declared Niyazov president for life.

President Saparmurat Niyazov, whose term of office will last indefinitely, asserts total authoritarian rule over Turkmenistan.

GOVERNMENT

THE POLITICAL CLIMATE IN TURKMENISTAN has been shaped by two powerful historical influences: the traditional tribal social structure and the communist system of government that established Turkmenistan as a country and then collapsed.

Until the Soviet Union created the Turkmen Soviet Socialist Republic, the people living there, like the people throughout central Asia, identified themselves as either nomadic or settled. These divisions were economic, not national or ethnic and certainly not political. Nomads and settled people had lifestyles that best suited their individual and preferred methods of earning a living. Within these two broad divisions, people belonged to tribes and clans.

The Soviet method of running a country clashed with this existing structure. Moscow's approach was to assign people to collective units in the hope of breaking down family and ethnic ties and replacing those loyalties with allegiance to the Soviet state. The strength of tribal identities and ways of life that existed in Soviet Turkmenistan, however, proved particularly resistant to change and resettlement. The central administrators in Moscow found that collective farms formed according to tribal division were the best possible compromise. One result of this slight deviation in standard practice was that people in the countryside never lost their strong ties to their tribes, and their traditions and loyalties were easily reestablished after the fall of the Soviet empire.

Above: **The Arch of Neutrality in Ashkhabad Square.**

Opposite: **A revolving golden statue of President Saparmurat Niyazov sits atop the Arch of Neutrality. It rotates so that it is always facing the sun.**

35

An elderly Turkmen and his donkey walk pass the limousines of government officials in Ashkhabad; such is the juxtaposition and divide between the different strata of Turkmen society.

THE DEMOCRATIC PARTY OF TURKMENISTAN

When the Soviet Union disintegrated in 1991, the Soviet central Asian republics declared their independence from the government in Moscow. Though Turkmenistan was a nation that had just been given its freedom, it asserted its independence less enthusiastically than the others. Its ruling party took as its name the Democratic Party of Turkmenistan and officially broke away from the Soviet Communist Party. However, of the Democratic Party's 52,000 members, 48,000 were former communists. In addition, all the executive and legislative leaders of the pre-independence period remained in office. Of particular significance to Turkmenistan's future was the leadership of Niyazov, president under the Soviets and president for life of present-day Turkmenistan.

If democracy simply means that people are granted the opportunity to vote for their leaders, Turkmenistan is a democracy. However, if it also means that people are allowed to form their own parties and be elected in opposition to the party in power, Turkmenistan is definitely

The grand Turkmenbashi Palace in Ashkhabad.

not a democracy. The current government of Turkmenistan preserves the old Soviet way of ruling with its centralized power stemming from a one-party system. An opposition party, the Watan (meaning "Fatherland"), exists mostly in exile and is officially unrecognized. All candidates for legislative office must be approved by the president, who also appoints all judges.

Turkmenistan has a constitution that guarantees religious freedom, freedom of expression, the rule of law, and the right of peaceful assembly. Few rights can be taken for granted in Turkmenistan. In general the rights commonly associated with true democracies do not exist at all. All activities in the country, and especially those pertaining to law, politics, and religion, are limited to those approved by President Niyazov. Dissent, especially after an apparent attempt on the president's life in 2002, is a hazardous endeavor. Dissidents have been imprisoned, killed, and resettled in remote communities, following the example of the Stalinist policies of the USSR.

THE PARLIAMENT AND REGIONAL GOVERNMENT

Turkmenistan's two parliamentary bodies—the People's Council and the Assembly—are charged with many duties, such as passing laws, administering government agencies, and calling elections. Their primary and overriding duty, however, is to approve and support the rules and proclamations of the president, in whom all power resides. To that end, in 1999 the parliament adopted an amendment to the constitution and proclaimed Niyazov president for life.

Five administrative regions (*viloyat*) are served by the central government: Akhal, Balkan, Dashhowuz, Lebap, and Mary—in which 20 cities and 46 towns are located. Each *viloyat* is divided into a number of districts (*etrap*): Akhal (eight *etrap*), Balkan (six *etrap*), Lebap (13 *etrap*), Dashhowuz (eight *etrap*), and Mary (11 *etrap*). These regions and districts are administered by officials who are either appointed by the national government or elected with its approval.

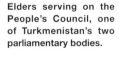

Elders serving on the People's Council, one of Turkmenistan's two parliamentary bodies.

ELECTIONS

The government of Turkmenistan strongly encourages all people over the age of 18 to vote, as much to show support for the system as to choose representatives, who must first be approved by the government before they can run for office. Despite such incentives as free towels and candy at the polls, it is not unusual for people to decline to vote. When the government finds that voter turnout is too low, poll workers carry the ballot boxes from house to house. Additionally, people unable to go to the polls can choose a representative to vote in their place. This practice can result in artificially high voter turnout figures. In the event that no one person achieves a majority, which can happen when there are multiple candidates running for the same office, a runoff election between the top candidates determines the winner.

As the people are often embroiled in their daily affairs, voter turnout in the republic tends to be low.

SAPARMYRAT TÜRKMENBASY ADYNDAKY AEROPORT

The Ashkhabad Airport
carries the name of
Turkmenistan's leader,
President Saparmurat
Niyazov.

ASHKHABAD

Ashkhabad, the nation's capital, has a long and complex past. In the first
century B.C., the small wine-producing town was leveled for the first time
by an earthquake. Nearly 2,000 years later, in 1948, an earthquake once
again flattened the town, killing two-thirds of its people. In the years
between the two earthquakes, the growing urban center was at times
an important outpost along the Silk Road, where caravans stopped to
unload and reload as their goods made their way across central Asia. At
Ashkhabad the routes divided, and caravans could continue their trip
either along the northern leg, which wound through the mountains,
or they could head south to an alternate road through the desert. The
city survived under the name of Konjikala until the 13th century when

the Mongols destroyed it on their rampage through central Asia. In the following centuries, it was a seasonal nomad camp until the Russians arrived in the 19th century.

Because of its convenient location on the Russian-built Trans-Caspian Railway, and because of its closeness to Persia and the absence of resident Turkmens to potentially complicate the situation, the planners and architects of Russia's expanding empire saw Konjikala/Ashkhabad as an ideal settlement. Building from the ground up, they had established a European-style city of more than 100,000 people when the earthquake of 1948 leveled Ashkhabad once again.

Housing in Turkmenistan is architecturally varied, with styles reflecting the different facets of Turkmen experience and history.

GOVERNMENT

The word *Ashkhabad* means "City of Love," though not many would find that phrase an accurate description of the capital's current state. With its population of about 550,000 people, Ashkhabad sits at the edge of the desert before the sprawling backdrop of the Kopet-Dag mountain range. Its buildings reflect a blending of various architectural styles: flamboyant structures built to glorify Niyazov, Western-style hotels built to draw the tourist trade, huge Soviet-style apartment blocks, and traditional Turkmen brick houses. It is also the site of many museums and, of course, government palaces and ministries. Green parks provide relief from the heat of the encroaching desert in the summer months, and the city maintains its tree-lined streets.

Railway passage between Turkmenistan and Uzbekistan was impeded following the attempt on President Saparmurat Niyazov's life in 2002.

INTERNATIONAL ISSUES

After the apparent assassination attempt on the life of President Saparmurat Niyazov in 2002, which the president blamed on the Uzbeks and which Uzbekistan in turn claimed was staged by the Turkmens, relations between Turkmenistan and Uzbekistan became hostile. With Turkmens and Uzbeks living in both countries, the tensions were magnified and borders were closed, making passage between the two countries inconvenient or impossible. Trade ceased, and harsh words came from both sides for more than two years. In late 2004 President Niyazov accepted an Uzbek invitation for a state visit to Tashkent, Uzbekistan's capital, where leaders from both countries met and mended fences.

When the former Soviet republics of central Asia became independent in the early 1990s, many expected they would form favorable trade

President Saparmurat Niyazov meets Afghan president Hamid Karzai *(left)* and Pakistan's then prime minister Mir Zafarullah Khan Jamali *(right)* in 2002 in Ashkhabad. They met to discuss the prospect of a gas pipeline that would connect and benefit their native regions.

President Saparmurat Niyazov *(third from the right)* joins the leaders of the Commonwealth of Independent States in Moscow for its annual summit in May 2005. Despite attempts at greater visibility and inclusiveness, the Turkmen leader still asserts absolute sovereignty over the country that he has effectively isolated from the international arena since he took office in 1991.

alliances with one another and adopt policies that would allow for the easier flow of people and goods across their various borders. This has not proven to be the case. Turkmenistan and its neighbors have struggled to establish working economies amid deep-rooted poverty and corrupt or totalitarian rule. The now independent republics have expressed little desire to work together in framing their economic policies and maximizing their individual potentials.

Still, Turkmenistan is attempting to gain greater international visibility through its membership in various organizations. It belongs to the United Nations, is a member of the Commonwealth of Independent States (CIS), and is part of the North Atlantic Treaty Organization's (NATO's) Partnership for Peace.

For some people from other countries, Turkmenistan's gestures of goodwill have only gone so far. Western governments and humanitarian organizations, including the United Nations, have found Turkmenistan's abuses of human rights troubling and have criticized the Niyazov regime. International environmentalists strongly object to the effects of Turkmen activities in the regions bordering the Caspian and Aral seas. Still, Turkmenistan's willingness to allow the United States to set up Turkmen military bases in order to gain access to Afghanistan during its war against the Taliban, has earned it favor in Washington, D.C. Prior to the terrorist attacks on the United States in September 2001, Turkmenistan had recognized and supported the Taliban.

RUHNAMA

Many of President Niyazov's theories of life and his interpretation of Turkmenistan's history are contained in his two-volume work, *Ruhnama*, or *Book of the Soul*. The first volume was published in 2001 and contains not only Niyazov's own life story but also his version of Turkmenistan's history and the moral lessons to be learned from it. The second volume was published in 2004 and addresses family values and patriotism.

The first volume of the *Ruhnama* has been required reading for all Turkmens since its publication. Excerpts are inscribed over the doors and on the walls of mosques, and President Niyazov has declared it to be a sacred text to be studied and read alongside the Koran. It is the main text in all classrooms, where students read it at the beginning of every school day. In many classrooms, it is the only text. On Saturdays adults are required to study the *Ruhnama* as well and to contemplate spiritual matters. The month known as September in the English-speaking world is called *Ruhnama* in Turkmenistan. Niyazov is also the author of two other books that enjoy wide circulation in the country: *May the Turkmen People Be Blessed* and *The Five Centuries of Turkmen Spirituality*. He is also a poet, and state television affords Turkmens many opportunities to hear him recite his verse.

Turkmenbashi greets a group of young admirers, raised to revere their leader.

TURKMENBASHI, SAPARMURAT NIYAZOV

Turkmenistan is ruled by a former Soviet official who came to power in 1985 and has ruled ever since. Born in 1940, Saparmurat Niyazov is a Turkmen and a member of the Teke group. Trained as an engineer, he served the former USSR in several capacities before being appointed the head of the former Turkmen Soviet Socialist Republic. In his career under Soviet rule, he was one of the most conservative officials. He resisted reform measures and glasnost, an easing of the once stiff restrictions governing people's lives, even as these reforms were starting to go into effect in the Soviet Union. Despite a written constitution that declares Turkmenistan to be a democratic republic with a balance of power divided among its three governmental branches—executive, judicial, and legistative—Niyazov rules as a virtual dictator. He has allowed the legislature to make his presidency a lifetime appointment and has adopted the name Turkmenbashi.

The name *Turkmenbashi* means "Father of all Turkmens," and President Niyazov has taken it upon himself to offer fatherly guidance to all of Turkmenistan's nearly 5 million citizens. He has lectured young people on their appearance, telling them to give up the long hair, beards, and multiple gold teeth that had become fashionable. He has banned smoking in public places as a result of his own experience with heart disease. The test for a driver's license includes demonstrating knowledge of appropriate moral principles derived from the *Ruhnama*. The president believes these moral principles will guide his people to drive not only safely but also with consideration for other drivers and for pedestrians.

The *Ruhnama*, the president's self-penned spiritual guidebook, contains the principles and ideals to which every Turkmen is expected to adhere.

Opposite: **A guard is stationed in front of one of the many statues of Turkmenbashi found in Ashkhabad.**

Below: **This portrait in Ashkhabad was replaced when Turkmenbashi had his hair dyed black.**

Many of Niyazov's other policies governing the lives of his people are less paternal. Dissidents have been imprisoned in psychiatric hospitals and threatened even in exile. Illegal dissident behavior includes reading a foreign newspaper, practicing an unacceptable religion, and listening to forbidden broadcasts. Government functionaries have been fired and prosecuted for not meeting agricultural goals. College degrees from foreign nations are no longer recognized in Turkmenistan, leaving few educated people and qualified personnel available for assuming teaching, health care, and even government positions.

In 2002 Niyazov was the target of an assassination attempt. As part of the investigation and the purges it subsequently triggered, more than

1,000 people were arrested and convicted in trials that were either conducted in secret or for public display. Civil rights and freedoms were suspended. A new law imposed further restrictions on movement and personal expression. Disobedience to and a deviation from this law would result in heavy penalties such as the seizure of property and forced labor. Activists were required to register with the government or face prosecution. It is now considered treason to express dissatisfaction with the president or his government.

The image of Niyazov crops up everywhere in Turkmenistan. A golden statue in Ashkhabad revolves in the city center, 39 feet (12 m) high atop a 246-foot (75-m) pedestal, turning its face to follow the sun's direction. Towns and streets bear his name as do several of the nation's schools and airports. A meteorite was even named after Niyazov to extol his family name and lineage. His likeness is featured on the country's currency, and his portrait appears at all times, even revolving like the statue, in the corner of the television screen. Occasionally, it has been necessary to make adjustments to the thousands of portraits found throughout the country, as in 1999 when he dyed his white hair black.

ECONOMY

AS A SOVIET REPUBLIC, Turkmenistan's contribution to the Soviet economic system was far greater than any support it received. During the years of Soviet control, Turkmenistan was one of the poorest of the republics. Today it is still one of the poorest of the former Soviet republics. With the onset of independence, little has changed. Poverty remains one of the nation's major challenges.

ECONOMIC PROMISE

Turkmenistan is rich in mineral resources. Large oil and natural gas deposits lie along the coast of the Caspian Sea. In the early days of independence, Russia, the United States, and other countries explored the possibilities of building pipelines to transport natural gas through Iran and Turkey to Western markets. However, political events and uncertainties have postponed and possibly permanently prevented any progress. The government continues to explore potential pipeline partners in an effort to broaden the market for its gas. Until it can build a pipeline to the south, though, it is locked in a hostile partnership with Russia based on a pipeline network established prior to independence. The poor economic conditions of Turkmenistan's trading partners, mainly former Soviet republics, have made price adjustments difficult for them to absorb as well.

Officials are also trying to develop the nation's other mineral resources, which include coal, sulfur, salt, phosphate, iodine, and lignite. In addition, Turkmenistan's gypsum and limestone have proved plentiful sources of building materials, for both domestic demand and export.

Irrigation makes the cultivation of barley, sesame, millet, corn, and wheat crops possible, as well as vegetables, melons, grapes for wine, and

Opposite: **Beneath the smooth sand and seemingly barren landscape of the Kara-Kum Desert lies Turkmenistan's wealth. The country's oil and natural gas reserves are among the largest in the world.**

alfalfa. The main agricultural crop, however, is cotton, which is grown along the canal through the desert and at oases near the Murgab and Tedzhen rivers. Turkmenistan is one of the world's 10 largest cotton producers. The government sets very high goals for the production of cotton, and though children and soldiers become part of the crew at harvesttime, cotton output has rarely exceeded one-third of its projected goal.

Regardless of whether the cotton yield meets its production objectives, the crop has done little to benefit the farmers, students, and soldiers who harvest it. Schoolchildren, taken out of their classes; college students, whose tuition goes to waste as they perform the difficult manual labor; and soldiers, working for very low wages, all unwillingly take jobs from farmers who find themselves competing with people working for little or nothing.

More than 90 percent of the land under cultivation is irrigated, drawing water from the Aral Sea. The same level of irrigation activity that was established under Soviet rule is maintained, though the water in the Aral Sea is dangerously diminishing and the area's freshwater supply is threatened as well.

FARM ANIMALS

Domesticated animals are a source of labor and products for Turkmenistan, with cattle and sheep supplying much of the region's meat, and horses and camels serving as work animals. Karakul sheep and silkworms are raised for the wool and silk they provide for Turkmenistan's rug weavers.

The Karakul sheep may well be the world's oldest domesticated breed. Carvings of the Karakul have been found on ancient Babylonian temples

Young Turkmen women display the fruits of their labor in one of the many cotton fields found along the rivers of Turkmenistan. Cotton is one of the country's principal exports.

dating back to 1400 B.C. Their skins were highly prized by traders on the Silk Road. The Karakul is native to central Asia, where it has thrived in the dry desert at high altitudes. Over the centuries, the harsh conditions of its home environment have bred exceptional hardiness into the Karakul. Its sharp teeth last long into old age, enabling it to forage in the scarce vegetation of the mountain deserts. Able to survive in the extreme heat and cold, Karakul sheep also possess a strong flocking instinct, and the mothers are attentive to their lambs. Both these traits are advantageous to the sheep as they travel long distances twice each year.

The Karakul sheep is called a fat-tailed sheep, a distinction that is more than just cosmetic, because its tail stores fat. The fat provides nourishment,

Carvings of Karakul sheep have been found in the ruins of ancient Babylonian temples.

much as the camel's hump does, in the marginal land where few other animals can survive. A ewe can have as many as three lambs each year. The lambs are born with a curly, glossy black coat. In North America, these coats are known as Persian lamb and were once the height of fashion for coats, jackets, and hats. The garments were made from lambs slaughtered no more than three days after birth. On lambs fortunate to live longer, the curl relaxes as the sheep reach adulthood and their coats change color. The adult coat contains both long silky fibers and a coarser layer of guard hairs that can be used in both woven and felt materials. Adult Karakuls can be brown, gray, and sometimes even white.

The silky fur of Karakul lambs is especially valued but the wool, meat, milk, and fat of the adult sheep are equally precious to the thrifty nomadic Turkmens, who for centuries have moved their households to take the sheep to fresh pasturelands. The sheep have provided homes, tools, furnishings, and clothes as well as food for the Turkmens. It is little wonder that the people of Turkmenistan and much of central Asia developed a lifestyle in response to the life cycle and needs of the sheep.

INDUSTRY

Turkmenistan's industries are related to its mineral and agricultural products and include meat and fish processing, petroleum production, oil refining, the making of textiles, and the quarrying of building materials.

THE TRANS-CASPIAN RAILROAD

A cooperative endeavor between Iran and Turkmenistan resulted in a rail link being established between the two countries from the border city of Sarakhs to Mashhad in Iran. The route began operating in 1996

Passengers on a train in Ashkhabad. The opening of the Trans-Caspian Railroad linked Europe and Asia in an effort to revive the Silk Road, the network of trade routes that once threaded through the central Asian region.

and has both cultural and economic significance. Trade between the two countries has been made cheaper and faster as a result. In addition, the Turkmen populations of both countries have benefited from the increased ease of travel.

ECONOMIC GROWTH

Among the legacies of Soviet rule is a bureaucratic and administrative tendency to misrepresent or inflate economic growth. In 2004, as in previous years, the government announced that the economy grew more than 20 percent. However, this number does not reflect any improvement in the standard of living for individual Turkmens in reality. The government has refused to share the bases for this economic statistic with international observers, claiming that the numbers are state secrets. Additionally, differences between local and international accounting methods can result in varying conclusions. One conclusion all observers and participants agree on, however, is that the president controls Turkmenistan's resources and sets goals for all of the nation's economic sectors.

As in the Soviet years, some industries and sectors are encouraged at the expense of others. The production of cotton, initiated by the Soviets, continues to dominate the Turkmen economic system. The Soviet planners saw the sparsely populated country of Turkmenistan as the cotton bowl for its textile industry, and with good reason, since the republic alone supplied most of the cotton used in the USSR. Today cotton is still an important cash crop, but the organization and distribution system that the Soviets established proved difficult for the new government to replace or copy. A coherent system of production that can supply jobs, equipment, education, and health care has not yet taken hold.

Numbers and government claims do not tell the complete story of the economic status and well-being of any society, but in Turkmenistan the

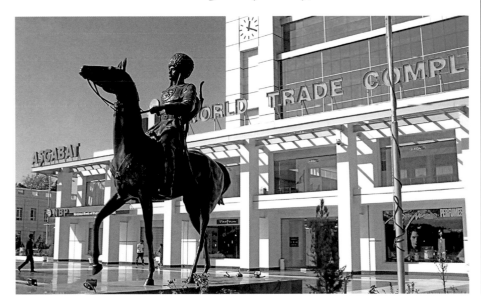

The World Trade Complex in Ashkhabad.

story is more complicated than most. Since independence, the Turkmen government has claimed it has supplied free gas, electricity, water, and salt to all its citizens. In theory, this would raise the standard of living for Turkmens, though the improvement would not be reflected in their level of income. However, the reality is that the government pays little for these products and services, so the suppliers charge their major corporate customers hefty rates and fees instead. The effect is that while the people have the supplies and basic necessities, the cost of doing business in Turkmenistan discourages investors on both the local and international levels.

A Turkman entering a taxi in the midst of heavy traffic in the city.

TOURISM

The government, through its State Committee for Tourism and Sport, seeks to encourage tourism in Turkmenistan by drawing the world's attention to its carpets, its fabulous Akhal-Teke horses, its lively music and dance traditions, and its growing number of hotels. At international trade shows, the products and performing arts that make Turkmenistan attractive are on open display, and visitors are drawn to the possibility of travel there. Unfortunately, also on display and heavily promoted are various translations of Niyazov's *Ruhnama*, a stark reminder of an overbearing and egomaniacal dictatorial presence that could potentially discourage tourists.

A tour bus rumbles along a road winding through the arid and mountainous terrain of the Kara-Kum Desert.

ENVIRONMENT

FOR MORE THAN 50 YEARS, preserving the health of the environment has not been a top priority for the leaders of present-day Turkmenistan. The current officials continue to elevate the short-term needs of the economy over the necessity of halting or curbing the devastation caused by uncalculated agricultural practices.

A SHRINKING LAKE

The Aral Sea is located north of Turkmenistan, between Uzbekistan and eastern Kazakhstan. Environmentalists around the world know that Lake Aral, as the body of water is sometimes called, is in danger of disappearing altogether because the rivers that flow into it are being drained for irrigation and for water consumption by people living not only in the surrounding areas but also in distant lands. Shortsighted Soviet planning drained the rivers for years to irrigate desert cotton fields, resulting in the contamination and drying up of the lake. Besides the loss of water and the threat to wildlife that the lake supports, pesticide contamination is also harming the area's human population. In addition, the Soviet biological-weapons research station—where scientists experimented with and disposed of viruses and other bacteria in the hopes of developing biological weapons—now lies abandoned on Vozrozhdeniya Island in the Aral Sea. As the Aral Sea shrinks, Vozrozhdeniya is no longer an island 124 miles (200 km) long, but has become a peninsula 1,242 miles (2,000 km) long that connects to the shore of the lake. Though the Soviets had promised to clean up the

Above: **A ship in permanent dry dock, stranded on a strip of exposed land that was once covered by the Aral Sea.**

Opposite: **An aerial view of what was once the extent of the rapidly disappearing Aral Sea.**

area, Russia has not followed through and has, since the collapse of the USSR, blamed the central Asian governments for the damage instead.

In 1950 the Aral Sea was the fourth largest lake in the world, surpassed in size only by the Caspian Sea, Lake Victoria, and Lake Superior. Fourteen cubic miles (60 cubic km) of water drained into it from the Amu Darya and Syr Darya rivers. Fifty years later, after the Soviets had turned central Asia into their own private cotton basin, diverting and draining the rivers in the process, the Aral Sea receives only 0.3 to 1.2 cubic miles (1 to 5 cubic km) a year. Scientists maintain that 8.4 cubic miles (35 cubic km) are needed just to stabilize the shoreline. The surface area of the waters has shrunk from 258,234 square miles (66,900 square km) to about 11,966 square miles (31,000 square km). Scientists estimate that 75 million tons (68 million metric tons) of salts and dust blow off the exposed seabed, reaching as far as the Himalayas, Belarus, and the Arctic Circle.

The effect on the wildlife of the region has been catastrophic. Of the more than 20 species of fish once living in the lake, only two survive, and just 38 of the 178 animal species native to the region remain. Through the years, the climate has become even more extreme, with hotter summers, colder winters, and increasing dryness.

With the surrounding countries still economically dependent on the nation's massive cotton crop, the demand for water shows no sign of lessening. Most likely, the lake will continue to shrink and salinized land, or soil with a high salt content, will continue to emerge. To make matters worse, drums full of contaminants had been dumped into the lake by the Soviets on Vozrozhdeniya Island. Scientists testing the sands and water have determined that, though treated with bleach and dumped into trenches, the spores of many of the contaminants have survived.

There is more and more evidence of the devastating impact pollution and environmental abuse have had on the region. It comes in the form of the various illnesses and abnormalities afflicting the native residents. Inhaling pollutants and drinking water containing between seven and 16 times the acceptable level of pesticides and other pollutants, the people suffer from anemia, birth abnormalities, shortened life spans, and more frequent occurrences of malignant tumors and infant mortality.

As the Aral Sea continues to shrink, the effects of contamination are expected to only worsen, while nothing is being done to limit the impact on Turkmenistan or any other country that draws on the rivers that supply the sea's water. As the salinized area of the seabed becomes increasingly a part of the land that once surrounded the lake, the toxins dumped by the Soviets and, since 1991, the surrounding central Asian states, are likely to be further dispersed by rats and other scavengers through direct contact and water contamination. Devastating outbreaks of smallpox, anthrax, typhoid fever, plague, and other medical disasters loom in the future for the people of the region if immediate action is not taken.

The supply of valuable and once plentiful Caspian caviar is quickly being depleted.

ENDANGERED STURGEON

More than 90 percent of the world's beluga caviar, the most highly prized caviar, which is made from the eggs of the sturgeon, comes from the Caspian Sea where the fish has lived since prehistoric times. However, fishermen have said that the already high price of $830 per kilogram of eggs is going to go even higher as the supply dwindles. Before long, some experts predict, the fish eggs may not be available at all as the fish comes closer and closer to extinction. Since the fall of the Soviet empire, fishing has been unregulated and unmanaged in the former Soviet republics of Turkmenistan, Azerbaijan, Kazakhstan, and Russia. With national economies struggling and unemployment high, poorer people and caviar smugglers have been unrestricted in what they harvest from the sea. Smugglers consider the dangers and risks of being caught and imprisoned well worth the price of their "black gold," and thus trade flourishes. Finding the nine- to 18-year wait for the fish to mature and produce the eggs insufficient in offsetting their prevalent and persistent poverty and hunger, poor fishermen catch the fish for its meat.

A painting of people repairing nets off the coast of the Caspian Sea where fish used to be in abundant supply. The Caspian Sea's fluctuations in depth and area, due in part to the building of dams and canals in the region, are of serious concern not only to environmentalists but to the fishing and shipping industries as well.

TURKMENS

OFFICIAL POPULATION STATISTICS for Turkmenistan are not easy to find, since there is no general agreement. The government of Turkmenistan gives the figure as 6.5 million, but most international observers put the number between 4.8 and 5 million. The population of Turkmenistan is 85 percent Turkmen, 5 percent Uzbek, 4 percent (and falling) Russian, and the rest Armenian, Kazakh, Tatar, and Ukrainian. It is a youthful population: 36 percent of the people are under 14, largely because of a high birthrate (nearly four children for every woman) and a low life expectancy. Families are generally large: nearly one-third of them have seven or more members. Fewer than half of Turkmenistan's people live in urban centers, with 55 percent living in rural settlements in the river valleys or the desert.

Left: **A Turkmen family poses in front of its home. Large families are common.**

Opposite: **Rural Turkmens tend to be self-sufficient and highly adaptable. Here, a Turkmen woman holds some cotton, Turkmenistan's prized cash crop, while a companion looks on.**

Turkmen elders with their traditional woolly hats gather for a chat in the town square.

TRIBES, GROUPS, AND FAMILIES

Though it is not certain what their origins are, the Turkmens (the ethnic majority in Turkmenistan) most likely came to central Asia from the remote eastern steppes around 2,000 years ago. Today they live primarily in Turkmenistan, Uzbekistan, Iran, northern Iraq, and Afghanistan.

The main groups are the Yomud, from the western and northern parts of the country; the Teke, found today living around Ashkhabad; and the Goklan, whose lands stretched to the west of Ashkhabad. Historically, the nation's major tribes were independent of one another, each keeping to its own territory and maintaining a unique culture and distinct dialect. Interaction among the tribes led to shared traditions of art and jewelry styles. Still, each tribe distinguished itself from the others by retaining unique features and qualities, such as different weaving patterns and clothing styles, especially when it comes to headgear.

The structure of the individual tribes was complex and varied somewhat in terms of leadership and authority, though urban, rural, and nomadic families alike showed great regard for their elders. Tribes were further divided into groups and then into extended families, the basic unit of social and economic organization. Most families were self-sufficient, living off the products of their livestock herds as well as a little farming.

Marriage was and remains central to Turkmen society, traditionally because of the need for workers. Within the tribal system, women were the weavers and were responsible for milking the cows and sheep and preparing the dairy products so crucial to the family's diets. In settled communities, women also often helped plant and harvest crops. However,

Women have proved a vital and necessary force in the household as well as the economy at large.

most important of all, they gave birth to and raised the children. Even today, a large family commands respect and admiration, which is why elaborate courting and wedding ceremonies are still among the most celebrated Turkmen social events.

Turkmen society was different from most other Muslim societies. Although Turkmen women were usually not visible participants in political affairs, they were never required to wear face veils or were subject to strict seclusion. Their specialized and necessary roles and skills made them vital contributors to the economy, not just beneficiaries of it. Under Soviet rule, state ideology dictated equality between the sexes. Because of its Turkmen tribal traditions, the population of Turkmenistan was able to adjust to the major social change other cultures and societies found radical and offensive.

Still, during their years as citizens of a Soviet republic, Turkmens saw their culture trivialized, degraded, and ultimately replaced by rigid and uncompromising Soviet ideals. So encompassing was the communist ideology that uprooted the Turkmen way of life that the years since emancipation have been shaken by questions of identity and values. The unpredictable rule of President Niyazov has not simplified this identity crisis, since conflicts between religion and government have trickled down into conflicts between tribes.

RUSSIANS

During the Soviet years, thousands of Russians relocated to Turkmenistan. Many were sent by the central government in Moscow to fill administrative, government, teaching, and other professional positions. Functioning in this capacity, they formed a prestigious and influential class of their own

within the country of Turkmens. After the breakup of the USSR, the Russians were increasingly considered outsiders, though they held dual Russian and Turkmen citizenship. They were no longer welcomed by the new government, despite the fact that the government itself consisted largely of former Soviet leaders. Turkmenbashi, in particular, wished to rid his country of people potentially disloyal to him. In 2003 he terminated the dual citizenship of the 100,000 remaining Russian-Turkmens, giving them 60 days to choose which affiliation they would keep. Rather than giving up their Russian citizenship or living as Russians in the Turkmen nation, many fled to Russia. Since then, Turkmenistan has become even less hospitable to its Russian population, banning all Russian media, removing Russian studies and language from its schools, and declaring college degrees granted from Russian institutions of higher learning, and in fact from all foreign universities, invalid.

In a Turkmen village, a young girl gives her little brother a ride in a wheelbarrow. Under the leadership of Turkmenbashi, the quality and availability of education for rural children have sharply declined. The president decides education policy and determines the nation's curriculum standards himself.

LIFESTYLE

WITH UNEMPLOYMENT PAINFULLY high, Turkmenistan could be a country with an overwhelming number of starving, homeless citizens. However, the government provides its people with goods and services that are guaranteed by the constitution: housing, medical care, education, and leisure. In addition, the constitution guarantees gender equality and the right to choose one's marriage partner. Obligations include mandatory military service for all men and the payment of taxes as the government assesses and dictates. The constitution also grants the right to freedom of religion, fair trial, legal retribution against unlawful government activity, and freedom from forced testimony and torture, but these rights are frequently and conveniently overlooked.

All media in Turkmenistan are strictly under the control of the government, which funds radio and television stations and owns all printing facilities. Editors of all newspapers and magazines are appointed by President Niyazov, who also directs their editorial content. Newspaper stories consist, for the most part, of the president's speeches and proclamations and the glorification of his various deeds and achievements. What space remains is filled with positive stories about holidays and Turkmens who display the attitudes and attributes that the president wishes to promote. Turkmens have not been traditionally drawn to reading newspapers, so it has been necessary for the government to require that its officials subscribe to the country's papers in order to maintain a respectable circulation. Foreign newspapers and magazines were banned in 2002, and shipments are often confiscated at the borders.

Turkmens have the choice of watching programs from one of four television stations. Each of these is controlled by the government. About 10 percent of the programming is news, which consists entirely of

Opposite: **A picture of ceaseless activity and bargaining, the bazaar in the Kara-Kum Desert is a common place for Turkmens to shop and sell their goods, much less exchange news with friends.**

material promoting the programs and ideologies of the government. The rest of the schedule is filled with folk music performances and patriotic programs that explain the president's books and his key beliefs. Russian programming is strictly limited and censored, and consists mainly of children's shows. Some people have satellite reception to access Russian broadcasts, but this is considered risky.

Journalists, both Turkmen and foreign, who contradict government expectations can expect harassment for themselves and their families and may experience difficulty in obtaining visitors' visas.

DRESS

The typical Turkmen woman wears a long dress called a *koynek*. It is a nearly floor-length garment often made of silk woven on narrow looms. Because the fabric is so narrow, the dress is cut straight with full-length triangular inserts in the middle, giving the dress a graceful flair at the bottom. The circular neckline is decorated with contrasting embroidery in brightly colored silk. The embroidery is usually done by the woman who owns the dress or by her mother as part of her dowry. Under the *koynek*, the woman wears pants called a *balak*, sometimes made of several kinds of fabric. Only the silk-embroidered bottom border of the *balak* shows beneath the *koynek*.

A Turkmen man will often wear loose-fitting blue trousers stuffed into tall heavy boots. Over this, he traditionally wears a white shirt covered by a heavy silk jacket with red and golden stripes. Both men and women wear distinctive headgear. A woman always has her hair pulled back, often in braids, and covered by a scarf. For special occasions, she will typically put on an elaborate headdress that shows off the jewelry that constitutes her family's wealth. A man's hat will often reveal what tribe he belongs to, and the most commonly seen style looks like an explosion of fluffy wool.

Traditionally, people removed their shoes before entering a yurt, whose inhabitants tended to walk, sit, and sleep on the felted rugs that covered the floor. Indoors, individuals wore knitted slippers or socks called *joraps*. Usually made of soft lamb's wool, but sometimes of

silk or cotton, the socks were usually covered with geometric or floral designs representative of a particular area.

Young people have been inclined to dress in Western-style clothing. Long hair, piercings, and gold teeth are also popular. However, such styles and fashions are discouraged. Turkmenbashi has declared them unsuitable for Turkmens and has urged young people to dress in traditional clothing. Women are being told to return to the long pants and outer dress of the past. For a number of reasons, people have complied with these suggestions: first, because it is dangerous to disregard their leader's suggestions, and second, because the national costumes display traditional artistic skills and tribal identities.

Turkmenbashi takes it upon himself to dictate the fashion trends of his people, discouraging such things as the gold teeth this woman displays.

FAMILY STRUCTURE

The extended family is the central social unit of Turkmen society. People usually marry quite young, often in their teenage years. Traditionally, the groom's family pays a bride-price in the form of either animals and goods or cash to the bride's family. The woman leaves her family to live with her husband's family in his father's household. When a man is in his 30s, he leaves his father's household with his wife and children and forms a household of his own. He takes with him part of his father's wealth and establishes his own independent livelihood.

A man's work, in nomadic and rural settlements, takes him away from home quite often. His responsibilities center on farming, caring for livestock (including sheep shearing), and going to the market. A woman's work includes child care, food preparation, and the spinning, dying, and weaving of wool.

Despite the incursions of the government, family is one of the most important and defining institutions in Turkmenistan.

77

High-rise apartment buildings are one of the legacies of Soviet rule.

HOMES

Turkmenistan is a country of cities as well as rural settlements. The cities, many of them built in their present form under Soviet rule, have housing typical of the former Soviet republics. Large block-style apartment buildings, as well as single-family mud-brick houses are common sights in the smaller towns. Palatial buildings line the streets of the neighborhoods of Ashkhabad where government officials make their homes and their fortunes.

For centuries, though, the nomadic lifestyle of the Turkmens dictated a very different kind of residence. Living alternately in areas of extreme heat and extreme cold, Turkmens needed shelter that would suit both climates and that was portable as well. Their land had few trees for building houses, and stones and mud bricks were not very portable.

Hence, the yurt: a portable dwelling, circular in shape, and about 16 feet (4.9 m) in diameter. Its collapsible walls and roof were standard shelter for nomads, and even settled Turkmens often kept a yurt for summer living. The latticework walls of the simple structure were covered with felt or reed screens to create an impromptu home.

LIFE IN A YURT

Everything the nomadic Turkmens owned or needed had to be moved at least twice a year and unpacked, reassembled, or installed on arrival at the new location. Decorative objects were a luxury, so weavers made practical, everyday items such as sacks, packs, rugs, and pillows beautiful as well as useful.

The woven bag was a staple of the Turkmen household, usually highly specialized according to its size and use. There were bags for carrying tobacco, spindles, tent poles, tea, flour, seeds, and bread. Bags hung on both sides of camels and horses, toting bedding, clothing, and pots.

Besides bags, the yurt was furnished with carpets. The dirt floor of the yurt was covered first with felted rugs that formed a soft warm surface for people to walk and sit on. The inside walls were lined with woven carpets that served as decorations by day and bedding by night.

Under the high central wheel, which allowed air to circulate, was a stove used to prepare food for the family and to heat the yurt in winter. In front of the stove, a specially shaped rug kept sparks from falling on the other rugs and coverings. The stove was framed with mud bricks or wood in a square 3 feet (0.9 m) on each side. Radiating from the stove, the interior of the yurt was divided into four sections.

Near the doorway in the front of the yurt, people left their shoes, tied up small animals, stored stools, and received ordinary guests. Behind the

The portable yurt can be easily assembled and dismantled, giving the nomadic Turkmens added mobility.

stove was the family's sleeping area and the place where they received guests of distinction. There the family stored or hung on the wall the main carpet—a pile (or tufted) rug that they unrolled when they had guests. Most other rugs in a yurt were flat-woven coverings. At night the family slept in a row along the back of the tent. The men slept on one side and the women on the other, all on their own sleeping felts, covered with their own quilts, their heads pointing toward Mecca.

The work area for men was on one side of the stove; the women's work area was on the other. Both were furnished mostly with the equipment needed for the various tasks they performed. Depending on the tribe, the assigned side for each sex could be to the left or to the right of the central roof opening.

The women's side was known as the pot side, and all supplies needed for cooking were stored on posts or trestles high above the ground. Other supplies such as sheers, spoons, and bedding were laced to the walls in bags specially designed for them. One bag held dirty clothes, and another stored clean clothes.

The men's side was known as the provisions side. There the family stored salt, grain, rice, and other dry foods in paired bags that hung on both sides of the camels during travel. Newly shorn fleeces and unused tent felts were stored on the men's side as well.

THE MARKET

Traditionally, the people of central Asia did their buying and selling in outdoor markets, not in stores housed in permanent structures. The markets

A vendor sells her wares at a bustling Sunday market.

were usually temporary but scheduled, and people traveled at regular intervals to trade their wares. Today the remnants of these huge markets are still active in some towns and villages. One market, the Tolkuchka, located outside Ashkhabad, is typical. Open Sundays and Thursdays, it is a place where Turkmen jewelers and weavers come to sell their wares to countrymen and vistors alike, haggling with them all in turn.

EDUCATION

With more than 36 percent of Turkmenistan's population under the age of 14, education in the nation is a major concern. But the system has undergone substantial revision since independence. The requirement for attendance has declined from 11 to 9 years, though in reality few children attend even that long. The school year has been shortened, schools are closed during the cotton harvest so that children can work in the fields, Russian has been removed from the curriculum along with all books written in Russian, and the main textbook in all classes is Turkmenbashi's book of moral principles and mythologized history, the *Ruhnama*.

The schools themselves are crowded and largely unheated. Teachers earn around $60 per month, but they are often not paid for months at a time. They must provide their own classroom supplies, such as pencils and paper and any other text they wish to use besides the *Ruhnama*.

College education within Turkmenistan is limited to two-year degrees, leaving even the most educated Turkmens with less than the equivalent of a high school education. Even with the lower requirement for graduation,

One of the few major cotton exporters of the world, Turkmenistan maximizes its output of the crop by soliciting the labor of the people during harvesttime.

Turkmen students making their way to school in the desert breeze. Both education and health care inadequacies in Turkmenistan have been attributed in part to the lack of trained teachers and medical personnel.

the number of students entering college has fallen from more than 40,000 per year under the Soviets to fewer than 4,000 in 2003 when the government began charging tuition. Students from poor and rural families were especially burdened. Many still lived in local economies where payment is made through trading goods rather than in cash. Students studying abroad are also unlikely to return to Turkmenistan now that their degrees will not enable them to find jobs back home.

HEALTH CARE

Health care in Turkmenistan is free for all citizens, though it is largely unavailable in areas outside the cities. In April 2005 President Niyazov ordered all of the hospitals located outside the capital to be closed. Under Soviet rule, poorly trained workers and underused health-care facilities burdened the economies of its republics. These republics have struggled to pay for health care since independence. Turkmenistan's solution has lowered costs, but it has also reduced the availability and quality of services. Claiming that health-care workers suffered from a mindset that valued self-interest over service, Niyazov fired 15,000 trained nurses and doctors in 2004, and replaced them with individuals drafted into the military. The government also prohibited workers from reporting cases of infectious disease.

Turkmenistan's medical laboratories and treatment facilities are outdated even in the cities and are not available in many rural areas. The death rates of mothers and children under the age of 5 are the highest in all

Turkmenistan's infant mortality rate has risen, especially in the rural regions, as people are increasingly deprived of proper medical care.

AGING IN TURKMENISTAN

The writings of Turkmenbashi have established the stages of life for his people. The ages of human life for the citizens of Turkmenistan are officially as follows:

Childhood	0–12
Adolescence	13–24
Youth	25–36
Maturity	37–49
Prophetic age	50–62
Age of inspiration	63–72
Age of wisdom	73–84
Old age	85–96

Turkmens who live to be more than 96 years old are now said to be living in "the age of the Oguz-han." Oguz-han was the Turkmen who is said to have died at 109. Turkmenbashi, born in 1940, has entered the age of inspiration.

of central Asia, especially in the areas affected by the pollution of the Caspian and Aral seas.

MILITARY SERVICE

All men are required to serve two years in the military once they turn 18. More than 100,000 men are drafted each year. Besides military service and training, conscripts are required to perform much of the work usually done by hired workers, such as road building and repair, health care, and

harvesting (especially cotton). Turkmenistan also maintains an internal security system. Though its size is secret, its effects are substantial, and Turkmens live under the assumption that their activities are being monitored.

INTERNATIONAL AID

For the first few years following the declaration of independence, foreign NGOs (non-governmental organizations) helped to fill the void left by the collapse of the Soviet system. However, increasingly, the government has made their work difficult. Each year more humanitarian workers leave the country, along with well-trained personnel, both foreign and Turkmen.

Boxes of gifts from children in the United States are delivered to Afghan children in Turkmenistan. Humanitarian groups have faced great hostility from the government of Turkmenbashi amid accusations of human rights violations raised against the administration.

RELIGION

HISTORICAL RECORDS SHOW that the area that would become Turkmenistan had more than 400 mosques in 1911. Then, under Soviet rule, the number fell to four. Today, the figure is hard to determine because the government opens and closes mosques according to terms not always clearly understood by worshipers, but estimates reach as high as 3,000. Ashkhabad is home to the largest mosque in central Asia. In design, it combines both the ancient and the modern styles of Islamic architecture. It has been criticized outside of Turkmenistan for the prominence it gives to Turkmenbashi and his writings, which are upheld with as much significance as are the words of the Koran.

Freedom to worship in Turkmenistan is guaranteed in the constitution, which says, in part: "Everyone shall have the right independently to determine her or his own religious preference, to practice any religion alone or in association with others, to practice no religion, to express and disseminate beliefs related to religious preference, and to participate in the practice of religious cults, rituals, and rites."

Like many rights guaranteed by the constitution, the freedom to worship is not practiced as set down in theory. The law states that religious groups must have 500 members where they wish to congregate and must register with the government. The only religions whose registrations have been accepted are Sunni Islam and Russian Orthodox Christianity, though other sects and faiths definitely have more than 500 members. People wishing to take part in unregistered religions are forbidden to gather publicly, distribute materials, or recruit new members. The government's interpretation of "public gathering" prevents meeting privately as well.

Religious intolerance in Turkmenistan, however, owes everything to the country's Soviet past and the present totalitarian administration, in

Opposite: **Turkmen elders praying in a village mosque in the Kara-Kum Desert. The majority of the population of Turkmenistan is Sunni Muslim.**

particular President Niyazov's desire to control the freedom of expression and worship in his country. It is quite foreign to Turkmen tradition, which, though overwhelmingly Islamic, has been notably tolerant and uninvolved in controlling or regulating the religious beliefs of others. Religious and national identity and motivation have been ranked behind tribal affiliation in importance. Religious oppression in Turkmenistan stems not from differences in spiritual belief, but from a fear of opposition to government policies.

ISLAM

Nine out of 10 Turkmens identify themselves as Sunni Muslims. Sunni Islam is a form of the religion that dates back to the disciples of Muhammad. While in some countries Sunni Muslims are quite explicit and rigid in their beliefs about proper behavior and modes of worship, Turkmenistan's Muslims have had to be flexible in the past to survive the Soviet antireligious regime. Today flexibility reigns as long as they share the teachings of their president in their mosques and incorporate these into their sermons.

Sunni Muslims believe in one God, whose word was conveyed to them by the Prophet Muhammad. Principles underlying the faith are referred to as the Five Pillars of Islam. The first pillar is the belief that there is no other god but Allah, the true God, and Muhammad is his messenger; the second pillar is a promise to pray to God five times per day; the third pillar commits a believer to serving and helping the poor; the fourth pillar requires Muslims to fast from dawn to sundown during the month of Ramadan; and finally, the fifth pillar is the expectation that all who are able to will travel to the holy city of Mecca in Saudi Arabia once in their lifetimes.

GOVERNMENT AND RELIGION

The government of Turkmenistan takes part in the religious climate of the nation in a variety of ways. For several years, just before Ramadan, the president has pardoned thousands of prisoners, releasing them from jail and allowing them to return to their homes. These are often people who have been jailed for trivial matters and are of no threat to society or to the regime. They are released simply on their promise not to reoffend.

The government also supports a limited contingent of pilgrims making the hajj, the journey to Mecca each Muslim tries to make once in his or her lifetime. Paying for passage and accommodations, the government allows more than 180 pilgrims to make the long trip each year. The

A remnant of an ancient Islamic structure, found outside Ashkhabad.

pilgrimage begins at Geok-Tepe, where the Russians massacred 15,000 people in 1881. Following a ritual meal, the pilgrims leave accompanied by prayers for peace, stability, and prosperity in Turkmenistan, which they carry with them to Mecca.

The government has had a negative impact on religion and congregations of the faithful in the nation.

By destroying places of worship— demolishing at least seven mosques in 2004 as well as Christian churches and Hare Krishna temples—the government has created a climate of fear and oppression. None of the demolished houses of worship has been rebuilt or allowed to reopen.

Another ancient mosque in Turkmenistan, testifying to the early influence the religion had on the future nation.

The famous Kipchak Mosque in Turkmenistan.

Niyazov built the Kipchak Mosque, reportedly the largest mosque in central Asia, in his hometown in central Turkmenistan. Even before its opening, the mosque had become controversial because quotes from Niyazov's *Ruhnama* adorned the walls with as much prominence as did quotes from the Koran. Many Muslims regard such reverence for the *Ruhnama* as blasphemous—that copies of the book are placed in mosques along with the Koran and that imams, or Muslim religious leaders, are instructed to quote from the president's writings in their sermons.

LANGUAGE

TURKMEN, THE OFFICIAL LANGUAGE of Turkmenistan, is a member of the Turkic family of languages, a group that also includes Turkish and Uzbek, as well as Kazakh, Kyrgyz, and Uighur. Many of these languages are like dialects of the same language—with similarities in syntactical structure and vocabulary. Most central Asians who speak one Turkic language can at least understand speakers of another. Still, there is a great deal of variety, and the 3.1 million people who speak Turkmen use more than seven dialects, including Yomud, Teke, Salir, Goklan, Arsari, and Chowdur. Each is associated with a specific tribe. The Yomud and Teke dialects have contributed the most to the official language, which was standardized in 1920. Other influences come from Arabic, Persian, and Russian from which words have been adopted and integrated into the Turkmen language over the years.

Turkmenistan is the geographical home and center of the Turkmen language, but more than a million of its speakers live outside the country. This is not surprising given the relatively recent establishment of borders often randomly dividing a previously nomadic population. Most people who speak Turkmen outside Turkmenistan live in Iran (with 850,000 speakers) and Afghanistan (with 700,000 speakers). There are significant populations living in Turkey, Uzbekistan, and Pakistan as well.

THE STRUCTURE OF TURKMEN

The common order of words in a Turkmen sentence is subject-object-verb. Words acquire meaning and context through the addition of suffixes. Suffixes added to nouns indicate gender and number or whether the word is singular or plural. Suffixes added to verbs indicate tense. The language

Opposite: **Two Turkmen women stop for a chat. Turkmen is identified by a majority of the population as their primary language.**

A road sign in Ash-
khabad.

has nine vowels, with both long and short sounds, and 23 major and two minor consonants. The vowel sounds of the suffixes and root words are always both long or both short.

WRITTEN TURKMEN

As a written language, Turkmen has a short history, but it has gone through many changes. From the 18th century until 1929, it was written using the Arabic alphabet, though little was actually recorded, and Turkmen was primarily an oral language. In 1929 an alphabet similar to and based on the Roman alphabet was introduced. The Unified Turkish Latin Alphabet, as it was called, was replaced by Cyrillic script (in which Russian is written) in 1940 to standardize Soviet communications.

WORDS OF THE TURK

Turkmen, Turkmens, Turkman, Turkoman, and Turkomans all refer to the group of people who originally came from the mountains of northwestern China. When it comes to the actual language, the word "Turkmen" refers to one language in Turkmenistan, a completely different tongue (Azerbaijani) in Jordan and Syria, and yet another in Tibet.

Below are some Turkmen words that are translated from the Turkmen alphabet into the Roman alphabet, or transliterated, so they can be pronounced as they are written. As in English, some ideas and actions can be expressed in many ways. The meanings of the Turkmen words for life and respect, for example, are numerous. Only familiarity with both the language and culture can help speakers know which word is most appropriate when used in a specific situation.

alphabet	*elipbiy*	mountain	*dag*
baby	*babek*	oasis	*oylyk*
beautiful	*ajayyp*	peace	*parahatchyly*
camel	*duye*	respect	*hormat, sylag, asgermek*
carpet	*haly*	Russian	*ors*
dictionary	*sozluk*	sheep	*goyun*
education	*magaryf*	shirt/dress	*koynek*
father	*kaka*	shoe	*ayakgap*
grandfather	*baba*	tea	*chay*
grandmother	*ene*	village	*oba, aul*
life	*omur, durmush, yashayysh*	world	*alem*
mother	*eje*	yes	*haw*

HISTORICAL AND CULTURAL SIGNIFICANCE

Tribal loyalties and tribal identification have historically formed the basis of the social and political structure of the Turkmens. The language of the Turkmens, with its dialects peculiar to each tribe but intelligible to all, was one of many ways people used—like the patterns in rugs and clothes—to associate an individual with a tribe or region. When the Russians conquered the tribes and imposed their rule, they also introduced their language and alphabet.

By the time the Soviet Union lost its power in 1991, most urban Turkmens spoke Russian, the language that government administration and business

were conducted in. Children learned Russian in school in addition to Turkmen, which was considered an inferior language to be used by those with no ambition. Still, as late as 1979, more than 99 percent of Turkmens claimed and regarded Turkmen as their first language. One of the first acts of the new government in 1991 was to proclaim Turkmen the national and official language.

Since 1991 political considerations have continued to strengthen the position of the Turkmen language as Russian influence slowly eroded. Once, Russian television and radio stations and publications encouraged the use of the Russian language. The Soviets had installed Russian officials in many government and teaching positions. These people found themselves unwelcome after the Soviet collapse, and many left the country. Today Russian broadcasts and publications are banned or severely discouraged, and classes are conducted entirely in Turkmen. Until 1991 there were universities and training schools in Turkmenistan operating in Russian, but these have been shut down. It has been difficult to reopen these schools with Turkmen as the operating language because there are few scholars educated in Turkmenistan.

Today English is considered Turkmenistan's second language, but the number of people who can teach it is decreasing. Turkmens educated abroad have brought English home with them, and in the early days of independence, Peace Corps workers from the United States and Christian missionaries from various countries gave the locals a chance to practice their English with native speakers. However, the government has since made foreign religious workers feel unwelcome, and its hostility toward humanitarian organizations and other NGOs has limited their presence as well. Likewise, since foreign degrees are unacceptable, fewer Turkmens will be studying abroad, and fewer scholars now abroad will be returning.

Above: **The teachings of the *Ruhnama* take precedence over academic subjects in the country's schools. Students often face the disadvantage of a persistent shortage of well-trained teachers.**

Opposite: **The nation's street signs, notices, advertisements, and billboards are written mostly in Turkmen.**

ARTS

FROM PREHISTORIC TIMES, the arts in Turkmenistan have been integrated seamlessly into daily life. Weavers, metalworkers, and potters made items that were both beautiful and essential to survival. Today many of these traditional arts continue to be practiced, though selling or trading has expanded the range of items once produced solely for domestic use. Music and literary arts are also closely intertwined, with poems and epics preserved in song.

Above: **Beautiful and popular Bukhara carpets for sale.**

Opposite: **Turkmen carpets are renowned for their durability and exceptional patterns and designs. They are exported to more than 50 countries around the world.**

FELTED RUGS

Though the rugs most often associated with Turkmenistan are woven, the most practical, and therefore the most commonly used, floor rugs are not woven, but felted. Used as bedding as well as floor coverings, these rugs are called *keshme*. For centuries, women made *keshme* for their families, and the rugs are still made in much the same way today as they were then.

Camel or sheep's wool provides the raw material for the *keshme*, and women provide the labor and artistry. Before a sheep is shorn, it is washed to remove as much dirt from its fleece as possible. After the shearing is complete, the women lay the fleece on the ground and beat it with sticks to remove any remaining dirt and to separate the fibers. When it is clean and separated, they dye it in batches in the colors that they will need for their designs. Traditionally, the dyes were made from plants and insects according to old recipes. Today the dyes are more likely to be commercially prepared from chemicals.

Women rolling a wool carpet as part of the felting process.

Ready for felting, the wool is then laid on a reed or straw mat in layers. The bottom layer is often undyed wool that is either dark or light, depending on the natural color of the sheep. On top of this, the women place tufts of dyed fleece in a pattern, building up the surface layer by layer until the design is complete.

The felting process is ancient and simple. Hot soapy water is sprinkled on the wool until the piece is completely soaked. Then the rug-makers roll up the rug, straw mat and all. With their forearms pressing on the rug, they roll it back and forth to press out the water and to cause the wool to fuse to itself. Sometimes they unroll the rug, sprinkle it again with hot soapy water, roll it up again, and press the piece some more. The resulting felted rug is strong, thick, and warm. The material is formed by the combination of heat, soap, and pressure in just the right proportions. The skills and the designs are passed on from one generation to the next.

Etiquette in a yurt requires that, before entering, people remove their shoes and put on slippers or socks. A felted rug provides a soft warm surface to walk and sit on. The thickness of the rugs also provides some protection from the scorpions and snakes of the desert. Besides the *keshme*, Turkmens also use felted materials for clothing and for the walls of the yurts themselves.

THE TURKMEN CARPET

The most acclaimed art form of the Turkmens is the woven carpet. Knotted pile or flat weave, the rugs and bags were traditionally created by women on horizontal looms set up in yurts. Wealthy families might have an entire yurt set up for weaving. Sheep were sheared in spring,

The National Carpet Museum of Turkmenistan is home to many samples of Turkmenistan's woven treasures.

and most families wove only the wool obtained from their own sheep. During the weaving season, after spinning the wool into yarn and dying it the colors needed for a particular design, the women spent almost all their time at the loom. They wove their patterns from memory, without charts or diagrams, often nursing their babies and instructing their older daughters in the weaver's art as they worked. Families that wove items for sale at a local market usually produced two rugs in a season. A young woman without children or other responsibilities could weave about 1 square foot (0.9 square m) in a 12-hour day. In wealthy families, for whom weaving was not an economic necessity, young women learned the skills and patterns that were part of their heritage as they wove the materials for their dowry and wedding ceremony.

No written account records the history of weaving, but archaeological evidence has suggested that weaving communities existed among some Turkmen tribes. Workers spun, dyed, and wove for the market that was created by the travelers and traders shuttling back and forth along the Silk Road. Within these communities, men sometimes wove as well and each worker specialized in one part of the process instead of working from sheared wool to finished carpet.

The Soviet years were a time of great change for the carpet weavers of Turkmenistan. To promote Soviet ideals, officials compelled the weavers to adopt a pictorial style that would portray and glorify the heroes and events key to the development of Communism. These carpets, known as theme or portrait carpets, were meant to be hung, rather than laid on the floor, and have deep complex borders along their lower edges.

Factories in Ashkhabad turned out countless numbers of huge carpets with Lenin's portraits. Fidel Castro (the leader of Cuba), astronaut Yury Gagarin, and Russian writers Aleksandr Pushkin and Maksim Gorky were rendered in tufted wool as well. In addition to Russians and key Communist figures, however, the weavers commemorated Turkmen literary giants, including Fragi Makhtumkuli, Kemine, and Mollanepes. Scenes portraying historical events and Soviet ideals, such as solidarity among workers, also became central themes, taking their place on stages and walls throughout the USSR. One particularly ambitious carpet entitled *Friends of the USSR Peoples* was woven in 1955 by a team of 25 Turkmen weavers. It shows the people of the USSR—men, women, and children in traditional dress—marching shoulder to shoulder with beaming faces. Above their heads waves a flag with the portrait of Lenin, as well as various banners of the Soviet Union. Surrounding the central portrait are many borders, some with *gul*, some featuring flowers, each more beautiful than the last.

In Ashkhabad, people can visit a carpet factory where 200 workers weave the traditional Bukhara carpet, known throughout the world for its dark red beauty and its extensive *gul* patterning. Visitors can watch the rug makers tying the tiny knots that form the dense pile that has softened the footfall of wealthy collectors and kings. Ashkhabad

Folk dancers and musicians perform on an interlocking spread of Turkmen carpets.

is also the site of the Carpet Museum, the permanent home of many beautiful carpets made by Turkmens, including the largest carpet in the world, which once graced the stage of the Bolshoi Ballet. There it hung as a backdrop to the dancers, reaching the height and width of the stage. Some of the portrait rugs that Turkmenistan's weavers produced during the Soviet years are also highlighted in the Carpet Museum, though many disappeared when Turkmenistan became independent.

The Bukhara carpet is the most famous of Turkmen designs, though it is named for the market where it was most often sold, in present-day Uzbekistan, rather than for the people who made it. Its main design element is the *gul*, the octagonal figure repeating across the width and length of the rug. Each tribe has its own signature *gul* and uses its hereditary *gul* in its weavings. Many carpets have two *gul* designs, one larger than the other and both repeating throughout the carpet. *Gul* identifying the five Turkmen tribes are featured along the left, or hoist, side of the official flag of Turkmenistan.

JEWELRY

In a culture that did not rely on money as a source of wealth, jewelry was traditionally the Turkmens' way of displaying affluence and social status. The valuable objects belonged to each woman, and they were hers to inherit and pass on, hence keeping much of the family's wealth under her control. Silver and gold ornaments were also created to decorate horses and riding equipment, such as reins, bridles, whips, and saddles. Only the most dire economic circumstances would cause a family to sell its jewelry. Unlike weaving, which was practical as well as attractive, jewelry making was an art practiced entirely for its beauty.

Most Turkmen jewelry is made of silver, often coated with a thin layer of gold and set with precious and semiprecious stones, especially carnelian, whose shades of red figure in so much of Turkmen art. Turkmen jewelers are typically men who have studied under older master jewelers to learn the techniques and patterns associated with their tribe. Artisans use designs exclusive to their tribes, with some using a wider range of stones and others doing without the gold coating altogether. Often the stones and the designs carry meaning as well as beauty, symbolizing joy, hope, healing powers, or strength of character.

The jewelry that a woman wears depends on her marital status and the occasion. A single girl wears an embroidered cap that has silver bangles and a pointed top. A married woman wears a high headdress that shows what tribe she is from. It is often decorated with a curved beaten silver plate. The top of the headdress might be adorned with as many as 100 pieces of jewelry, with more hanging from the sides. The most elaborate jewelry is worn by a bride and includes a headdress, bracelets, rings, necklaces, and silver bangles for her hair. A bride from a wealthy family might be wearing approximately 30 pounds (13.6 kg)

Elaborate pieces of jewelry, some encrusted with precious stones.

of jewelry at her wedding. Usually, a bejeweled woman wears pieces with dangling bangles that jingle as she moves.

Each item of jewelry has a specific name. One common piece, worn for many different occasions, is the *asyk*, a silver amulet (charm) that can either be attached to a woman's braids so that it hangs down her back or worn on a necklace as a pendant. The *asyk* can vary in weight from just a few ounces of silver to more than 5 pounds (2.2 kg). Another piece, the *tumar*, is a triangular bracelet worn high on a woman's chest or arm. The *tumar* has spiritual significance for Turkmens and often has a hollow tube for storing talismans.

LITERATURE

The origins of Turkmen literature are in the songs (*destan*), fairy tales, and poems (*epo*) that were passed on by the *bakshi* as part of the oral tradition that was common to many cultures in the region. The story of Koroglu is the oldest Turkmen song. Koroglu is an epic consisting of 209 verses. Selected verses are accompanied by music. Traditional instruments include the lute, flute, and single-reed pipes.

The Turkmen poet Makhtumkuli was and still is so highly regarded in his homeland that his work and life are celebrated with a national holiday on May 19, called the Day of Revival, Unity, and Poetry of Makhtumkuli.

Makhtumkuli's times and those of his fellow Turkmens were harsh with conflict not of their own making. The poet saw his and his compatriots' suffering as the cruel gift of fate. In his lifetime, he witnessed the Turkmen tribes at the mercy of the warring empires—the armies from Iran, Bukhara, and Khiva (now part of Uzbekistan)—that swept through their territory numerous times. No matter who occupied their lands, the Turkmens were consistently considered the invading force's enemies. Villages were sacked and burned, men massacred, and women and children carted off as loot. Some cities, such as Mary, were destroyed and rebuilt several times, and dams and oases were repeatedly ruined, leaving behind famine and barren, desertlike conditions.

A woman wears traditional Turkmen headgear.

To Makhtumkuli the world was a place of nightmares, where the clubs of the enslavers triumphed because of the disunity that reigned among the Turkmen tribes. He longed for a powerful confederation of tribes to throw off the burden imposed by the joint domination of the outsiders and warring native leaders. However, he never believed this hope would be realized, which was the ultimate source of his despair. He died without seeing the end of tribal warfare and the ousting of the foreign invaders. Yet his voice spoke to his people, and as a poet writing in their language, he was heard by the largely illiterate Turkmens who could recite all of his poems by heart.

Today Makhtumkuli has many followers with conflicting beliefs. Turkmenbashi has named a month of the year after him and devoted a national holiday to him. He also uses the poet's words to reinforce his calls for national unity. Though not openly uttered in Turkmenistan, other admirers of the poet-philosopher consider Turkmenbashi to be exactly the type of ruler as those who oppressed Makhtumkuli and the people of his day were.

Shadrdy Charygulyyev is a contemporary writer who has been a part of the literary scene since the Soviet days. His first collection of poems, *Bahar Gakylygy* (*The Call of Spring*), was published in 1979 and celebrated the themes for which he has become famous in Turkmenistan: love for his homeland, friendship and family, and natural beauty. Most of the works he produces as a poet and short-story writer have been for children, and he has been the editor of magazines for young readers under past and present regimes. Today he is the editor of *Gunes*, a children's magazine that is the government-approved successor of several other magazines. As such, it is popular among children and parents alike. In 2004 the government honored Charygulyyev for his conscientious work over the years.

Rakhim Esenov is a novelist and journalist who has been forbidden to leave the country since suffering a stroke following interrogation. He was arrested in February 2004 as he tried to smuggle 800 copies of his banned novel *Ventsenosny Skitalets* (*The Crowned Wanderer*) into the country. Written 10 years earlier, but banned because of what Turkmenbashi called historical errors, the novel was finally published in Russia in 2003. Its hero is Bayram Khan, a Turkmen poet, philosopher, and military hero of the 16th century. Esenov was charged with using the mass media to incite social, national, and religious hatred, charges that could bring him four years' imprisonment and confinement to the city of Ashkhabad to await trial. Unable to leave the country for essential medical treatment, Esenov has been recognized by the International PEN community of writers as one of the imprisoned writers of the world, and his dangerous situation has been a focus of the group's support.

TRADITIONAL MUSIC

Folk music is essential to the Turkman wedding and the festivities that surround it. One group of musicians that has attained international renown is Ashkabad, led by singer Atabal Tshaykuliev.

Local musicians perform in traditional Turkmen costumes.

He has been singing at weddings since the 1970s. He spent some time imprisoned in an asylum during the Soviet years for singing music that was considered too religious. Freed in 1985, he performs today with his band mates who accompany him on an astonishing variety of instruments, only some of which—including the violin, piano, accordian, clarinet, and soprano saxophone—are familiar to Westerners. However, the band's true sound is determined by the central Asian instruments they play—the *tar*, *serp*, *nagora*, and *dep*. The band's roots are eclectic and include classical Western music, jazz, and rock as well as traditional Turkmen music.

LEISURE

THE GOVERNMENT OF TURKMENISTAN is extremely concerned with how its people spend their leisure time. On the one hand, there is a great deal of leisure time, with joblessness freeing more than half the people from a traditional workday, and dwindling education standards occupying less and less of young people's time. On the other hand, many of the pastimes that people take for granted in other countries are forbidden to Turkmens, who are strongly urged instead to attend to their spiritual needs as guided by the *Ruhnama*. In Turkmenbashi's second volume, newly introduced to mosques, schools, and workplaces, the nation's president pays special attention to the needs of young people. These, according to his definition, include everyone under 37.

Above: **Passersby stroll by stalls on a street in Ashkhabad.**

Opposite: **Children playing in a park in the capital.**

To advance his spiritual agenda, Turkmenbashi has banned smoking, chewing tobacco, loud music coming from cars, and movies. Nightclubs must close at 11 P.M. Women are encouraged to wear the traditional, long embroidered dresses and headscarves and reject Western styles of clothing. The president also believes that higher standards of conservatism will better serve Turkmens, who will reap the rewards of spiritual superiority in the 21st century.

So far, the president's warnings have had little or no effect. Joblessness and drug abuse have afflicted the young people of his country. Alcohol use has also become common among a specific group: urban males. Though Islam forbids the use of alcohol, this is one of the areas where some Turkmens subscribe to their own form of the faith.

As in all things, the presence of President Niyazov is felt in the words of the national anthem, which pays tribute to the dedication of the Turkmens to the land of their ancestors as well as to the country's neutrality and its leader.

SPORTS

The concept of leisure as enjoyed by people on vacation or traveling for pleasure is new to most Turkmens, who have traveled mainly for economic and survival reasons and do not take vacations. Still, under the leadership of President Niyazov, who has a taste for lavish projects, the government has developed some elaborate centers dedicated to leisure activities. He is currently building an ice palace in the desert and has approved plans for a ski resort in the Kopet-Dag Mountains, near Ashkhabad.

NATIONAL ANTHEM OF THE INDEPENDENT, NEUTRAL TURKMENISTAN

The national anthem (music by Veli Mukhatov) is an important feature of many Turkmen gatherings, including services at mosques. Unlike most national anthems, it glorifies the president as well as the country. While extolling Turkmenbashi, singers of the anthem effectively declare their passion for their land and pledge their allegiance and loyalty to their nation. The land of Turkmenistan is referred to as holy land, and the nation's neutrality is celebrated.

The first verse is repeated as a chorus after each of the following verses in this literal translation from Turkmen.

Refrain:
The great creation of Turkmenbashi,
Native land, sovereign state,
Turkmenistan, light and song of soul,
Live long and prosper forever!

I am ready to give my life for the native hearth.
The spirits of ancestors and descendants are famous for
My land is sacred. My flag flies in the world,
A symbol of the great neutral country.

My nation is united and in the veins of tribes
Ancestors' blood flows undying.
Storms and misfortunes of times are not dreadful for us.
Let us increase fame and honor!

Mountains, rivers, and beauty of steppes,
Love and destiny, revelation of mine,
Let my eyes go blind for any cruel look at you.
Fatherland of ancestors and heirs of mine!

During festivals and on holidays, people all over Turkmenistan celebrate by watching dancers and listening to music. Many dance and music troupes travel around the country to different festivals and gatherings, performing traditional and contemporary dances as well as reading, enacting, and singing songs from the *Ger Ogly* and other poems and myths, especially love poems. When the troupes perform, they wear beautiful traditional clothing and jewelry.

Turkmenistan's Kuliyev (in yellow) struggles to retain control of the soccer ball during the 2004 Asian Cup Group C finals in Chengdu.

SOCCER

Soccer is a popular game in Turkmenistan. The national team is a member of FIFA, the International Football Federation. Unfortunately, the president of the Football Association of Turkmenistan (FFT) is in prison, convicted of excessive religiosity, which has hampered the development of the team within the country. It has also hindered the team's role within FIFA, whose funding and support—amounting to $250,000 per year—is necessary for the team's survival. In return for its investment, FIFA requires television rights and that the team compete against other countries, both conditions of which have been lacking.

Still, the bright green uniforms of the Turkmen team appear often in the Kopet-Dag Stadium, where a field has been constructed to meet international standards for the sport. The FFT is under the control of the Ministry of Sports, which schedules its matches and determines how often it competes internationally. As a result of the games against other countries, children are developing an enthusiasm for soccer and, in cities especially, love to play informal games.

STUDENT AND WORKER SPORTS AND GAMES

Many of the nation's schools have teams for competitions in chess, volleyball, and tae kwon do. From these championships, it is possible for participants to go on to international competitions, especially in tae kwon do. Tournaments featuring the winners of regional contests take place six times a year. Each tournament consists of 100 athletes taking part in three kinds of martial arts, competing for belts at all levels. Winners go on to take part in the contest for the World Martial Arts Championship. Turkmenistan's participation as an Asian culture is reflected in the popularity of martial arts such as karate and kickboxing as well as tae kwon do. Table tennis is another popular sport in Asia that enjoys a large following in Turkmenistan.

Workplaces also form teams that compete in various games such as checkers and darts. Following a system of encouraging competition among labor collectives first established by the Soviets, workers compete within

Boxing is one of the few competitive sports Turkmens are allowed to participate in. The government imposes strict restrictions and regulations when it comes to participation in international matches.

Turkmenistan, with the winners going on to face champions from other former Soviet republics.

THE OLYMPICS

Turkmenistan has sent athletes to the Olympics since 1996, though it has not yet won any medals. In 2004 the Turkmen Olympic team sent nine athletes—six men and three women—to the summer games held in Athens, Greece. There they participated in boxing, shooting, weight lifting, swimming, track and field, and women's judo. The most accomplished of the athletes was shooter Igor Pirekeyev, who had been the 2002 Asian champion and placed seventh in the 2000 Olympics. All of these sports are also popular among students and workers.

A jubilant Turkmen team at the opening ceremony of the 12th Paralympic Games in 2004, in Athens, Greece.

HORSE SHOWS

Horseback riding is a source of national and personal pride in Turkmenistan.
The beautiful *Akhal-Teke* horses, represented by the best of the breed,
put on competitive displays and race at many national events, to the
delight of the spectators. The president himself is a proud horse owner,
and a picture of his prized steed, Yanardag, is on the state emblem.
Equestrian competitions are held throughout the country. As part of the
competitions, students and their riding masters demonstrate the art of
training horses and riders.

Equestrians can also take part in a horse trek that originates in a stable
on the edge of the desert. Riding purebred *Akhal-Teke* horses, they make
trips into the desert, the mountains, and the lakes region that would last
one to 15 days. The trek is conducted in the Turkmen style and involves
visits to old nomadic and oasis settlements.

FESTIVALS

FESTIVALS ARE COMMON in Turkmenistan, where people celebrate everything from independence to melons, from their leader's birthday to their nation's neutrality.

NATIONAL HOLIDAYS

February 19 is a double holiday honoring the flag and celebrating the president's birthday. In Ashkhabad and other cities around the country, fairs and parades fill the day with festivities. Flags and large banners with Turkmenbashi's picture are even more plentiful and prominent than usual.

On October 27, 1991, Turkmenistan declared its independence from the Soviet Union. Each year independence is celebrated on that day throughout the country with parades and festivities. In Ashkhabad preparations for the great parade that celebrates independence and honors the country's president begin months in advance. With luck, the weather is sunny, and people cheer in tribute to the man on the balcony, their leader for life. The Turkmen army marches through the marble square to salute their president, shouting, "Turkmenbashi! Turkmenbashi!" Next come the beautiful golden stallions of Turkmenistan, hundreds of them with their hooves painted gold, their riders clothed in golden sashes and traditional lambskin hats. The horses are followed by hundreds of children who dance around a huge model of President Niyazov while they chant verses from his book.

In 1995 Turkmenistan declared itself a neutral country, unaligned with the interests, military or otherwise, of any country. This decision was so

Above: **Servicewomen march during the annual celebration of Turkmenistan's independence and the president's leadership.**

Opposite: **Turkmenistan's Independence Day is celebrated with grand parades led by huge portraits of President Saparmurat Niyazov.**

Military tanks roll onto the parade square in honor of President Saparmurat Niyazov.

important to the leadership that it named one of the days of the week Neutrality Day. So it is no surprise that Turkmenistan also has a national Neutrality Day. December 12 is set aside for celebrations. Two large arches in Ashkhabad commemorate Turkmenistan's independence and its neutrality. One is at the entrance of the national museum, and the other welcomes people to the country's largest shopping center.

Two other national holidays commemorate historical events. On January 12, Turkmens mourn the day when their ancestors were defeated by the Russians at the Geok-Tepe fortress in a clash that took thousands of lives. It can also be a day to remember those killed in the 1948 earthquake. May 9 is a day of celebration, called Victory Day, in honor of the defeat of the fascists and the German surrender in World War II.

Melon Day and Water Day are also national holidays. In a desert country such as Turkmenistan, people say that "a drop of water is a grain of gold." Thus, honoring water and hoping for its continued abundance seem to come naturally to these celebratory people. The sweet watery taste of a melon—a musk melon or a cantaloupe—is a treasure to desert people as well. People wear traditional clothes and spend the day eating melons at fairs across the country.

RELIGIOUS HOLIDAYS

Kurban Bairam and Oraza Bairam are religious holidays. On Kurban Bairam, people sacrifice a sheep and prepare traditional foods for neighbors and relatives in honor of Abraham's willingness to sacrifice his son. On this holy day, they also sail into the air on grand swings erected for the purpose, believing that swinging on Kurban Bairam will cleanse their souls. Oraza Bairam is a day of fasting when people do not eat or drink until nightfall.

For the four weeks of Ramadan, Turkmens engage in introspection and daytime fasting. Like Muslims throughout the world, Turkmens celebrate the end of the fasting season with magnificent feasts and parties with family and friends, beginning at midnight on Id al-Fitr. Dressed in their finest traditional clothing, people dine at elaborately laden tables until dawn. Music is heard throughout the land, and everyone joins in the dances or, at least, applauds the revelers.

A man stands behind a heap of melons on Melon Day, a festival celebrated with fairs, parades, and the sale of freshly harvested melons.

NEW YEAR'S DAY

Turkmenistan has two New Year's Days, one celebrated on March 21, and the other celebrated on January 1. Festivities begin on December 31, or New Year's Eve. Tradition calls for people to dress in clean clothes, take out all the trash, clean the house, and return all items or money borrowed during the year. Most important, the family table should be loaded with rich and festive foods. When all these matters are taken care of, Turkmens are ready to welcome the new year, a critical observance, since custom states that the way you bring in the year will determine the way you will spend it. Guests arrive on New Year's Eve around 6 P.M. and continue to come until 5 A.M. as they make their rounds visiting friends and family. At midnight everyone goes out into the yard to greet the new year with fireworks for the children and champagne for the adults. Some families have a new year's tree decorated like a Christmas

A simple Turkmen feast in Ashkhabad.

HOLIDAYS IN TURKMENISTAN

January 1	New Year's Day
January 12	Memory Day
February 19	National Flag Day
March 8	International Women's Day
March 21	Novruz Bairam (religious)
April 6	Water Day
April 27	Horse Day
May 9	Victory Day
May 18	Revival and Unity Day
May 19	Holiday of Poetry by Makhtumkuli
May 25	Carpet Day

Kurban Bairam (religious)—three days a year according to the Islamic calendar
Oraza Bairam (religious)—one day a year according to the Islamic calendar

June 21	Day of the Election of the First President
July 10	Melon Day
July 14	Turkmenbashi Holiday

Ramadan—the ninth month, according to the Islamic calendar

October 6	Remembrance Day
October 27–28	Independence Days
November 17	Student Youth Day
November 30	Harvest Holiday/Bread Day
December 1	Day of Neutrality
December 7	Good Neighborliness Day
December 12	Neutrality Day

tree, but it is most likely an artificial one because trees are too scarce in Turkmenistan to be cut down for temporary decorations. Families and friends also give gifts to the children on this important day.

The second New Year's Day is called Novruz Bairam, which means "new day." Novruz is an Islamic festival and a celebration of the vernal equinox that predates Islam. It is an occasion for dancing, traditional competitions and games, and music. Street fairs and parades are staged throughout the country.

FOOD

THE TYPICAL TURKMEN DIET reflects the relative poverty of the people and the lack of advanced means of distributing and storing food. It is a diet high in bread and cereal products such as noodles. The few ways that exist to transport and store food restrict many vegetables to a brief harvest season, and poverty restricts the amount of meat and dairy products available. The resulting nutritional pattern is typically low in protein and oil, and high in carbohydrates.

The government has recognized the importance of a balanced diet and has taken steps to educate the public and to make a variety of fresh foods available. It has also distributed iodine to an iodine-deprived population and in this way has reversed an alarming trend toward iodine deficiency and the consequent thyroid enlargement.

Left: **A young Turkmen woman selling bread at a bazaar.**

Opposite: **A vendor sells fresh pomegranates at a Sunday market in Ashkhabad. The availability of fresh agricultural produce in the region is made possible by irrigation along the Murgab and Tedzhen rivers.**

A woman makes and sells bread straight from a traditional oven.

VEGETARIAN AND MEAT DISHES

Vegetarian dishes are plentiful and imaginative in both homes and markets, where vendors sell prepared foods such as vegetable-filled pastries and thin pancakes made with cornmeal. A hot dish, which is a cross between a soup and a hot cereal, often takes the place of a full meal. The mixture can consist of mung beans, cornmeal, and pumpkin or root vegetables; or rice and yogurt. It is not fancy, but it is filling and nourishing. Noodles are also plentiful and are the basis for many dishes to which cooks add whatever is fresh or on hand.

The most common meat is lamb or, more likely, mutton (meat from older sheep) or goat. It is used sparingly though. For festivals such as Eid-ul-Azha, celebrating the prophet Ibraheem's (Abraham's) faithfulness and willingness to sacrifice his son if God so willed it, those who have the means usually sacrifice a goat or a lamb to share with poor neighbors as well as extended family and friends.

RHUBARB

One of the most prized trade items on the Silk Road (*below, archaeological ruins at the ancient city of Merv, an important point and trade center along the Silk Road*) was rhubarb. From China where it was grown, it traveled along with silk, diamonds, and rubies and was considered just as precious. As famous a traveler as Marco Polo considered it valuable enough to include a bag of rhubarb in his will. For centuries it was used as an often necessary purgative and laxative. As late as the 19th century, a Chinese diplomat, desperate to stop the British from trading in opium, threatened to stop the sale of Chinese rhubarb to England. By that time, however, rhubarb was widely grown in England, and the British continued to sell opium to the Chinese.

EATING AT HOME

The economy of Turkmenistan has not flourished enough to support restaurants or the habit of dining out. However, eating is still a social event that brings families and clans together.

Preparing food gives women a chance to exchange news and teach their daughters how to prepare the dishes the family eats on a daily basis. Throughout the day, a kettle is kept boiling for tea, and visitors are offered tea and cookies if they drop in. While the guests sip their tea, the women prepare more food. No one leaves a Turkmen house without eating a meal.

ISHLEKLY (MEAT PIE)

1 cup milk
2 tablespoons sour cream
$^1/_2$ teaspoon baking powder
1 egg
flour

$^1/_4$ pound ground lamb
2 cups diced tomatoes, with the juice
2 diced onions
salt and pepper
3 tablespoons butter

Mix the milk, sour cream, baking powder, and egg in a large bowl. Add enough flour so that the mixture does not stick to the sides of the bowl. Divide the dough into two balls, one twice as big as the other. Pat or use a rolling pin to roll the larger ball of dough into a circle about $^1/_4$ inch thick on a pizza stone or pan. Mix the meat, tomatoes, onions, and seasonings in a different bowl. Spread the mixture evenly on the dough, leaving about an inch of dough clear around the edge. Roll out the remaining dough into a circle slightly smaller than the first. Place it over the meat mixture and press the edges together to seal in the meat mixture. Brush the top of the *ishlekly* with melted butter. Bake at 425°F (220°C) for 25 minutes or until the top is golden. Let it cool for a few minutes before serving it with green tea.

PILOV

Delicious varieties of *pilov*, or pilaf, are as numerous in Turkmenistan as extended families or clans are. Many versions of this rice-based dish rely on carrots to provide texture and richness of color. A sweet *pilov* is also made with dried apricots. On special occasions such as birthdays and weddings, men usually prepare the *pilov*—the only time that men cook. Then it is served on a large platter from which everybody eats. Turkmen *pilov* is made in a heavy iron pot, called a *cazon,* that can hold 8 quarts (7.6 l) of sizzling food. Turkmens use cottonseed oil for this dish, but the following recipe uses vegetable oil.

$1^1/_2$ pounds carrots
5 medium-sized white or yellow onions
1 clove garlic
$1^1/_2$ pounds marbled beef
safflower or corn oil

ground pepper
3 cups uncooked rice
2 teaspoons salt
6 cups water

Grate the carrots coarsely or julienne. Chop the onions into small pieces, mincing. Separate and peel the garlic clove. Cut the meat into 1-inch cubes. Pour the oil to a depth of 1 inch in a large, heavy pot. Heat the oil, then add the meat and garlic and cook for about 10 minutes until they start to brown. Add the onions and pepper. Five minutes later, add the carrots and stirring often, cook for about 20 minutes until they are tender. Add the rice, salt, and water. Cover the pot tightly and cook over low heat for about 20 minutes until the rice is tender.

A   **B**   **C**   **D**   **E**   **F**

KAZAKHSTAN

UZBEKISTAN

1

• Konye Urgench

*Sarykamyshkoye
Ozero*

Dashhowuz •

*Zaliv Kara-
Bogaz Gol*

DASHHOWUZ

2

• Turkmenbashi (Krasnovodsk)

BALKAN

Turan Lowland

Amu Darya

Cheleken •

Nebitdag •

▲ *Gora Arlang
(6,168 ft / 1,880 m)*

Aladzha •

• Koturdepe

• Gazanjyk

K A R A - K U M   D E S E R T

• Yerbent

Chardzhou •

3

**CASPIAN
SEA**

Dekhistan •

Kopet-Dag Mountains

AHAL

LEBAP

*Repetek
Nature
Reserve*

Atrek

Büzmeyin •

ASHKHABAD •

Nisa •

Margush •

Kara-kum Canal

Mary •   Merv •

Tedzhen

Bayramaly •

Yolötan •

Murgab River

MARY

4

N

IRAN

Meane Baba •
Altyn Depe •

*Badkhyz
Nature
Reserve*

Gushgy

GARABIL PLA

AFGH

5

MAP OF TURKMENISTAN

KAZAKHSTAN

H

Ozero Aydarkul

TAJIKISTAN

Gora Ayribaba
(10,299 ft /
3,139 m)

Gaurdak •

● Capital city
● Major town
▲ Mountain peak

Feet		Meters
6,600		2,000
3,300		1,000
1,650		500
660		200
0		0
Below		Sea Level

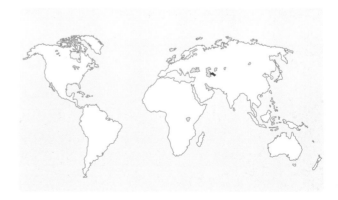

ECONOMIC TURKMENISTAN

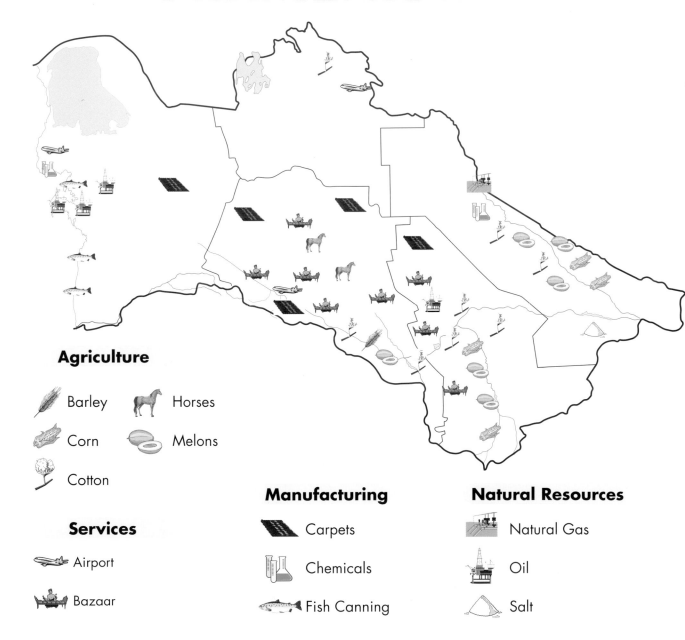

Agriculture

Barley

Horses

Corn

Melons

Cotton

Services

Airport

Bazaar

Manufacturing

Carpets

Chemicals

Fish Canning

Natural Resources

Natural Gas

Oil

Salt

ABOUT THE ECONOMY

GROSS DOMESTIC PRODUCT (GDP)
$27.6 billion (2004 estimate)

GDP PER CAPITA
$3,000; 58 percent living below the poverty line

GDP BY SECTOR
Agriculture 28.5 percent, industry 42.7 percent, services 28.8 percent (2004 estimate)

INFLATION RATE
9 percent

NATURAL RESOURCES
Petroleum, natural gas, sulfur, salt

PIPELINES
gas 4,069 miles, oil 866.8 miles

AGRICULTURAL PRODUCTS
Cotton, grain, livestock, melons

INDUSTRIAL PRODUCTS
Natural gas, oil, petroleum products, textiles, food products

CURRENCY
Turkmenistan manat (TMM)
USD 1 = TMM 5,200 (August 2005)

EXPORTS
Cotton, oil, gas, textiles

IMPORTS
Machinery, chemicals, food products

TRADE PARTNERS
Russia, Ukraine, Turkey, United Arab Emirates, Germany, China, Italy, Iran

WORKFORCE
2.32 million

WORKFORCE BY OCCUPATION
Agriculture 49 percent, industry 14 percent, services 37 percent

UNEMPLOYMENT RATE
60 percent

LITERACY RATE
98 percent

AIRPORTS
53; 23 with paved runways

PORT
Turkmenbashi

TELEVISION STATIONS
4, government-operated

TELEPHONES
Land lines 375,000, cellular 52,000

CULTURAL TURKMENISTAN

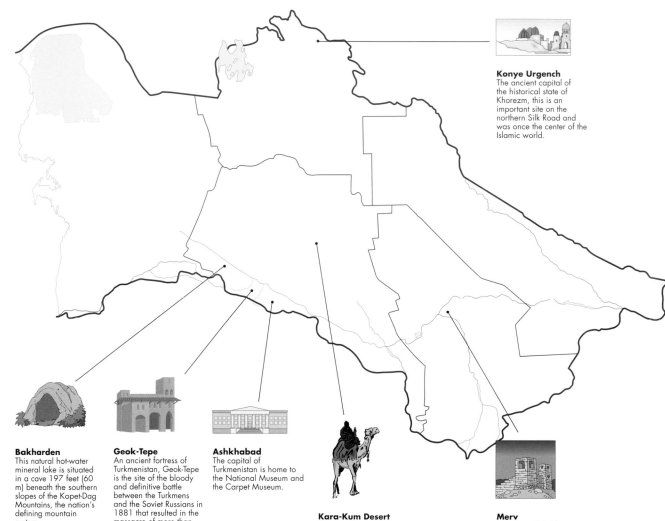

Konye Urgench
The ancient capital of the historical state of Khorezm, this is an important site on the northern Silk Road and was once the center of the Islamic world.

Bakharden
This natural hot-water mineral lake is situated in a cave 197 feet (60 m) beneath the southern slopes of the Kopet-Dag Mountains, the nation's defining mountain system.

Geok-Tepe
An ancient fortress of Turkmenistan, Geok-Tepe is the site of the bloody and definitive battle between the Turkmens and the Soviet Russians in 1881 that resulted in the massacre of more than 15,000 Turkmens and the establishment of Russian control of the area.

Ashkhabad
The capital of Turkmenistan is home to the National Museum and the Carpet Museum.

Kara-Kum Desert
This vast desert is home to the zemzen, a giant lizard also called a monitor lizard or a desert crocodile. It is known to eat many rodents and is cherished by Turkmens.

Merv
Listed as a World Heritage Site, Merv is home to ancient ruins dating to 6000 B.C. It was an important trading town on the Silk Road and was a slave-trading center.

ABOUT THE CULTURE

COUNTRY NAME
Turkmenistan

CAPITAL
Ashkhabad

TOTAL AREA
188,418 square miles (488,000 square km)

POPULATION
4,952,000

BIRTH RATE
27.68 births per 1,000 Turkmens

DEATH RATE
8.78 deaths per 1,000 Turkmens

INFANT MORTALITY RATE
73.08 deaths per 1,000 live births

LIFE EXPECTANCY
61 years

MAIN RELIGIONS
Islam and Eastern Orthodox Christianity

ETHNIC GROUPS
Turkmen 85 percent, Uzbek 5 percent, Russian 4 percent, others 6 percent

MAIN LANGUAGES
Turkmen 72 percent, Russian 12 percent, Uzbek 9 percent, others 7 percent

SIGNIFICANT PEOPLE
Saparmurat Niyazov (1933–), also known as Turkmenbashi, is appointed president for life. Fragi Makhtumkuli (1770–1840) is known as the "Father of Turkmen poetry."

THE TURKMEN FLAG
Created in 2001. On a bright green background, a red stripe runs from top to bottom along the left side. On the stripe are five *gul*, eight-sided carpet designs representing the five main Turkmen tribes. The designs are multicolored, combining white, green, orange, and red. Below them are crossed olive branches, similar to the branches on the flag of the United Nations. To the right, in the upper third of the flag, are five white stars representing the five administrative regions of the country, all cradled in a white crescent moon. President Niyazov has a flag of his own that often flies alongside the official national flag of Turkmenistan.

NATIONAL ANTHEM
"National Anthem of the Independent, Neutral Turkmenistan." Music by Veli Mukhatov.

TIME LINE

IN TURKMENISTAN	IN THE WORLD
	753 B.C. Rome is founded.
300s B.C. Alexander the Great conquers central Asia, including the area of present-day Turkmenistan.	**116–17 B.C.** The Roman empire reaches its greatest extent, under Emperor Trajan (98–17).
A.D. 600 Islam is introduced to central Asia as Arabs conquer the area.	**A.D. 600** Height of Mayan civilization
A.D. 900 Ancestors of Turkmens migrate to the area of present-day Turkmenistan.	**1000** The Chinese perfect gunpowder and begin to use it in warfare.
1200 Genghis Khan seizes control of parts of central Asia.	
1400–1800 Turkmenistan is ruled by Persians in the south and Uzbeks in the areas of Khiva and Bukhara.	**1530** Beginning of transatlantic slave trade organized by the Portuguese in Africa.
	1558–1603 Reign of Elizabeth I of England
	1620 Pilgrims sail the *Mayflower* to America.
	1776 U.S. Declaration of Independence
	1789–99 The French Revolution
	1861 The U.S. Civil War begins.
	1869 The Suez Canal is opened.
1881 Russians take over Turkmenistan following the Battle of Geok-Tepe, killing 15,000 Turkmens.	**1914** World War I begins.
1921 Turkmenistan becomes the Turkmen Soviet Socialist Republic.	**1939** World War II begins.

IN TURKMENISTAN	IN THE WORLD
	1945 The United States drops atomic bombs on Hiroshima and Nagasaki.
	1949 The North Atlantic Treaty Organization (NATO) is formed.
	1957 The Russians launch Sputnik.
1960s Turkmen cotton crop becomes central to the Soviet economy, beginning the destruction of the Aral Sea.	**1966–69** The Chinese Cultural Revolution
1985 Saparmurat Niyazov becomes leader of the Turkmen Communist Party.	**1986** Nuclear power disaster at Chernobyl in Ukraine
1991 Turkmenistan becomes independent with Niyazov as president.	**1991** Break-up of the Soviet Union
1992 Turkmenistan adopts a constitution.	
1999 Parliament makes Niyazov president for life.	**1997** Hong Kong is returned to China.
2000 Publication of the *Ruhnama*, a 400-page guide to good living, written by the president, which immediately becomes required reading for all Turkmens.	
2002 Niyazov survives an apparent assassination attempt and restricts civil liberties.	**2001** Terrorists crash planes in New York, Washington, D.C., and Pennsylvania.
2004 Second volume of the *Ruhnama* is published and becomes required reading in Turkmenistan's schools, mosques, and offices.	**2003** War in Iraq

GLOSSARY

Akhal-Teke
The Turkmen horse, a swift lightweight animal bred to survive the demands of desert life.

Arvana dromedary
A camel with just one hump, also called an Arabian camel.

bakhshi
A shaman or singer/poet.

etrap
A political district within a *viloyat* in Turkmenistan.

felt
A fabric made by matting protein fibers, such as wool or hair, using water, soap, and a great deal of rubbing or rolling.

glasnost
A Russian word referring to former Soviet president Mikhail Gorbachev's radical policy of openness and restructuring. It marks the beginning of moderate democratization of the Soviet Union.

gul
An eight-sided figure in a variety of designs used to identify a tribe and to decorate its members' belongings. The Turkmen flag displays the *gul* of the five major Turkmen tribes.

keshme
A felted wool rug or bed covering.

koynek
The traditional Turkmen woman's floor-length dress with elaborate embroidery around the neck.

nomad
A person who moves his or her residence seasonally within a defined area.

pilov
A rice dish with meat, fruit, or vegetables.

Ruhnama
This textbook of the Turkmens written by Turkmenistan's leader is required reading in schools, workplaces, and mosques. *Ruhnama* means "Book of the Soul" and is also the name of the ninth month of the year.

steppe
A partly or sometimes dry area where grass is the main natural covering.

Turkmenbashi
Means either "Leader of all Turkmens" or "Father of all Turkmens," the name President Niyazov has given himself.

viloyat
The regional political division in Turkmenistan.

yurt
A round tent, framed with lattices and covered in felted wool, a type of residence nomadic Turkmens have lived in for centuries.

FURTHER INFORMATION

BOOKS

Frank, Allen J. *Turkmen-English Dictionary*. Springfield, VA: Dunwoody Press, 1999.

Lerner Geography Department. *Turkmenistan (Then and Now)*. Minneapolis: Lerner Publishing Group, 1993.

Polo, Marco. *The Travels*. New York: Penguin Books, 1958.

Wood, Frances. *The Silk Road: Two Thousand Years in the Heart of Asia*. New York: University of Chicago Press, 2002.

WEB SITES

American Embassy in Ashkhabad. www.usemb-ashgabat.usia.co.at

Government of Turkmenistan (information about life in Turkmenistan and President Niyazov's pronouncements to his people). www.turkmenistan.gov.tm/index_eng.html

Human Rights Watch Organization (information about human rights issues in Turkmenistan). http://hrw.org/doc/?t=europe&c=turkmen

Peace Corps Web page. www.chaihana.com

Political Resources. Links to sites with information about the politics and history of Turkmenistan, including President Niyazov's home page, the CIA's page on Turkmenistan, and the Turkmen embassy's page. www.politicalresources.net/turkmenistan.htm

Turkmen International home page. www.turkmens.com

MUSIC

City of Love. Ashkhabad. Instrumental music from Turkmenistan. Clarinet, accordian, and fiddle supplement native Turkmen percussion and string instruments. Real World, 1993.

Instrumental Music of Turkmenistan. A recording of a concert by Turkmen musicians, called A Musical Voyage along the Silk Road. King Record Co., 1994.

Songs of Turkmenistan. Various artists. Folk music sung by Turkmen artists. World Music Library, 1997.

Turkmenistan: Songs of Bakhshi Women. Traditional vocal music. Silex/Auvidis, 1995.

BIBLIOGRAPHY

Klychev, A. *Carpets and Carpet Products of Turkmenistan*. Ashkhabad, Turkmenistan: Turkmen State Museum, 1983.

Mackie, Louise W., ed. *Turkmen: Tribal Carpets and Traditions*. Washington, D.C.: The Textile Museum, 1980.

Mayhew, Bradley, et al. *Lonely Planet Central Asia*. Oakland, CA: Lonely Planet Publications: 2004.

O' Bannon, George W. *From Desert and Oasis: Arts of the People of Central Asia*. Athens: Georgia Museum of Art, University of Georgia, 1998.

Wilson, Paul. *The Silk Roads*. Includes Turkey, Syria, Iran, Turkmenistan, Uzbekistan, Kyrgyzstan, Kazakhstan, Pakistan, and China. Hindhead, UK: Trailblazer Publications: 2003.

INDEX